I CAN'T HELP THE WAY I FEEL?

ROBERT AND GLORIA STELLA

EXPOSING THE *LIES* THAT *CONTROL* YOU

I CAN'T HELP THE WAY I FEEL?

Īedə,f ī

EDIFI PUBLISHING

Published by Edifi Publishing
3446 Winder Highway
Suite M195
Flowery Branch, GA 30542

info@edifipublishing.com
www.edifipublishing.com

Scripture quotations noted NIV are taken from the Holy Bible, New International Version, NIV®. Copyright © 1973, 1978, 1984, 2011 by Biblica, Inc.® Used by permission. All rights reserved.

Scriptures noted NKJV are taken from the New King James Version®. Copyright ©1982 by Thomas Nelson, Inc. Used by permission. All rights reserved.

Scripture quotations noted NASB are taken from the New American Standard Bible(r), Copyright © 1960, 1962, 1963, 1968, 1971, 1972, 1973, 1975, 1977, 1995 by The Lockman Foundation. Used by permission.

Scripture quotations noted WEB are taken from the World English Bible. The World English Bible (WEB) is a Public Domain Modern English translation and is not copyrighted.

Edited by Hannah Price
Reviewed by Amanda Walden, LPC
Cover design & layout by Gloria Stella
Author photo by Amanda Hamlin Photography

ISBN: 978-1-7339305-5-0

Printed and bound in the United States of America

10 9 8 7 6 5 4 3 2 1

CON TENT

INTRO DUCTION

"Thus says the Lord, the God of Israel,
'Write all the words which I have spoken to you in a book."

Jeremiah 30:2

This book came out of nowhere. One morning while we were working on other projects, God stopped us and directed us to prioritize this book instead. As we sat down - staring at a blank page - God quickly began to speak to us the words that now lay before you.

These words that follow may have been written pen to paper quickly, but they were developed in us over decades. Decades of believing the enemy's lie – that we "can't help the way we feel." Decades of "good" advice to "follow your heart." Decades of allowing a lack of self-control in our thoughts and emotions almost destroy the potential locked within our beings.

Decades followed by years of finally finding victory and healing. Years of discovering the keys to success in this area of our lives through God's Word. This doesn't mean that the occasional struggle doesn't knock on our door every now and again, but it means that we now know how to address it quickly so that we can stay the course of God's purpose for our lives – living abundantly and bearing fruit.

With all the trendy conversations circulating around accepting who you are, being true to yourself and the importance of self-care; what we lay out in the next few chapters aren't popular perspectives or thoughts. But we believe they are God's thoughts concerning your identity, your mental health and your relationships - and we believe God's way is the only way to achieve real victory.

We encourage you not to just read the words, highlight a few statements and set the book aside. You have to put it into practice. We can give you the seed of knowledge, but you have to be the one to plant it and consistently water it in order for it to yield fruit.

So grab a cup of coffee, a highlighter and a comfortable chair and dive in with us to expose this lie the world has taught us that we can't help the way we are, think or feel.

"GOD'S WAY IS THE ONLY WAY TO ACHIEVE REAL VICTORY.

\\ 1
IN THE WORLD

"For the wisdom of this world is foolishness in the sight of God."

1 Corinthians 3:18-19a

It's no secret that entertainment media is one of the largest influences in developed cultures. "Artistic works [are] often the most effective propaganda"[1] and organizations have used entertainment as a tool to indoctrinate nations towards specific agendas - and most of the time, we don't even realize it's happening. If humans can see the power of influence through media, then there's no doubt that the enemy utilizes it for his purposes as well.

Although we personally enjoy the entertainment value of many movies, it's difficult to deny the negative impact of desensitization. One of the most popular notions that has been cemented into our western culture through entertainment is the idolization of fairy tale romances. Marrying primarily for love is a relatively new concept to humanity – growing in popularity during the French and American revolutions.[2] In westernized cultures, it has now become the exclusive foundation of which the world – and the church - judges a romantic relationship.

I (Gloria) remember sitting in a theater back in 2004 watching the movie "Spanglish."[3] In the movie, there is a husband, a wife and a maid. The husband is a good-hearted guy who is genuinely trying his best to make his marriage work and make sure his children are loved. The wife is painted as a psychopath – she's cold, shallow, obsessive, selfish and borderline crazy. The maid is a beautiful single mom who is compassionate, understanding, smart and deserving.

The love story that the audience wanted to get was the happy-ending between the husband and the maid. It was a great love story and they would've made a beautiful family filled with love and happiness. However, at the end of the movie - before anything irreparable happened - the maid made the determination that she would not be "that woman" and she packed her bags, took her daughter and left. And the husband went back to his house with the crazy wife – who admittedly showed a sign of hopeful sanity at the close of the film. And that was it. The end.

I hated that ending. Inside, I was screaming "NOOOOOO!!!! Why did it end that way, that guy and the maid were perfect for each other and that wife is crazy and she doesn't deserve him!!!" It wasn't the happy-ending I wanted.

And then it hit me like a ton of bricks. At that time, Robert and I were intricate parts in establishing a Young Marrieds Sunday School ministry at our little hometown church. I advocated for marriages and the ability for God to restore any marriage – no matter how far removed. When did I get to the point that I allowed society to influence me so much that I would hope for the failure of a marriage in favor of emotional-bliss, even in the context of a movie?

It was the first time (of many) that God unveiled my eyes and I got a glimpse of how much culture influenced how we lived our lives. Even Christians living a Godly lifestyle are not immune to the unguarded influences of the world.

THE WORLD'S INFLUENCE

We are a society driven by our thoughts and emotions. We accept every thought that enters our mind as if they are our own thoughts and allow those thoughts to become "our truth" without further questioning. Our culture determines what the "right" decision is based on how we feel. We tend to live for the next emotional high – whether in a movie, someone else's life or our own lives. The dependence many of us have on our emotions to make us "feel alive" or "true to ourselves" has sadly left behind a trail of broken homes and broken people in its wake.

It's becoming difficult to take a look at what the world feeds us in movies, TV, music, tabloids and celebrated celebrity lifestyles and recognize that what is glorified is not truth; but rather, emotion. The world's obsession with pursuing and accepting their own feelings as fact is invading our lives at a rapid pace.

Although we live in the world, we are not of this world (Jn 17:16). But the more of this world that we consume intentionally or unintentionally, the more the world has an influence over the perspectives we have over our own lives.

BAD ADVICE

How many times have you heard of a friend seeking relationship advice who is immediately told to "follow their heart" or asked "what does your heart tell you?" How many times have you given that advice? It sounds like decent advice. After all, the generally accepted notion is that what's in your heart must be what's true, right?

But scripture says that the "heart is deceitful above all things... who can understand it?" (Jr. 17:9) and "out of the heart come evil thoughts, murders, acts of adultery, other immoral sexual acts, thefts, false testimonies, and slanderous statements" (Mt. 15:18-19). So to "follow your heart" is unpredictable and unbiblical advice. Although there may be the rare occasion that you feel the right emotions in a difficult situation, usually you feel the wrong ones. If that's the case, then how are you supposed to discern the difference based on your feelings alone?

Here's another example. How many times have you had a thought that goes against everything you've believed about yourself and immediately thought, "Why am I thinking that? What's wrong with me? Maybe that's who I really am?"

It doesn't matter what the thought pertains to – it could be an evil idea, a thought about your sexual identity, thoughts about your worth, thoughts about all the things that could go wrong, ideas of suicide, affectionate thoughts towards someone who is not your spouse, thoughts that confirm a bigoted attitude and the list goes on.

In this culture, most everything we do and believe comes from our persistent feelings or thoughts that eventually lead to the execution of those thoughts. People largely accept their emotions and thoughts without much question – after all, it's in their heart and their mind so it must be who they are. But not every thought or emotion originates from a person's core being – they can also originate from our carnality, from what other people have told us or from the enemy. We must constantly aware that thoughts and emotions are part of the arsenal of the enemy's "flaming arrows" (Eph. 6:16).

THE PROOF IS IN THE PUDDING

Most people would agree that you can tell how good something is working based on the results that are produced. If a genius marketing strategy is implemented but produces negative results, then the conclusion is that the strategy was wrong. It doesn't matter how trendy the strategy was or how excited everyone was about that strategy – the proof is in the pudding.

And yet, we live in a world where everyone pursues their own self-gratification and the realization of their emotions and their thoughts – good or bad. People want freedom and happiness and they think that if they can just "follow their heart" and "live their truth" unhindered, they'll find it.

But what has that led to? We are a generation filled with broken, depressed, anxious, sexually-confused, adulterous people with standards that fluctuate with every situation based on how we feel about it at that moment.

One of the most prevalent issues we see is the damage done to families because of emotionally-led decisions within marriages. Homes are torn apart because someone feels like they've "fallen out of love" with their spouse or they've "fallen in love" with someone else or many times – both statements are made in the same sentence. Those feelings have been placed above any and all sense of commitment or responsibility.

Our society makes destructive, life-altering decisions based on temporal and flippant emotions and the lack of perseverance to outlive or outgrow the temporary has led to a truly broken, devastated and immature society and people.

The world argues that the old antiquated teachings of the Bible are no longer true or relevant. The world teaches that if you "feel" something, you are indeed that "thing". You are living a lie if you feel an attraction but reject it. You're not "living your truth" if you desire, yet abstain from drinking or partying - regardless if your spiritual desire is to honor God with a holy lifestyle. Your anxiety is simply who you are and the world needs to adapt to you because you cannot change.

These are all lies and the enemy's attempt at shifting our focus off of God and back onto ourselves. Adam and Eve desired the tree; but had they maintained obedience, they would have lived a blissful and fulfilled life. It wasn't until they gave into their own feelings and desires and "lived their truth" that they failed and brought about misery for the world.

This isn't just in the world – this is in the church too. This cultural perspective of following your emotions or the direction of your strongest thought is something that we have dealt with in our own lives on multiple fronts and only by God's grace have we come to understand how we got into our messes and how to get out.

The world's strategy of doing what "feels good," "follow your heart," "be you," "do what makes you happy," "love yourself first" and every other popular self-focused hashtag you can think of - doesn't work. It hasn't produced genuinely fulfilled people. It's produced people with temporary seasons of happiness followed by seasons of greater emptiness. But this continuous cycle of emotional extremes is not what God intended. Rather, God desires to take us from glory to glory as we are transformed into His image (2 Co. 3:18).

We aren't saying that every emotion and every thought is wrong – many emotions and thoughts are right. But what is "right" can't be determined by emotions and thoughts alone and if our emotions and thoughts alone can't determine what is "right," than we certainly cannot live a life exclusively led by them. There has to be a higher standard of truth to which our emotions and thoughts are held accountable.

\\ **THERE HAS TO BE A HIGHER STANDARD OF TRUTH TO WHICH OUR EMOTIONS & THOUGHTS ARE HELD ACCOUNTABLE.**

\\ 2

THE

TRUTH

*"If you continue in My word, then you are truly disciples of Mine;
and you will know the truth, and the truth will make you free."*

John 8:31-32

Our emotions and thoughts are not in and of themselves "bad." We are not suggesting that everyone needs to live void of all emotions and free of their own opinions. It is not God's intention for us to have a lifeless existence or become robotic in our thoughts. Quite the contrary.

God created mankind as a "people I formed for myself that they may proclaim my praise" (Is. 43:21). God already has angels that praised Him – the difference with humanity is that He desired for us to choose to praise Him. He intentionally wants us to have our own thoughts and created us as unique individuals - each with "gifts that differ according to the grace given to us" (Rom. 12:6).

Our emotions are a gift from God – He put them in us so that we can live a life beyond data and facts. Being able to feel is a gift. Although there are a myriad of negative emotions - even those are required for us to be able to fully experience and enjoy the positive emotions. Emotions of joy, peace, trust, anticipation, excitement, friendship and laughter are just a sampling of the positive emotions that God wants us to experience.

The problem comes in when we combine our free will with the necessary negative emotions that we experience and then remove God's Truth. Our emotions are a gift from God, but if they are not given boundaries they will be used to destroy our lives rather than enhance it.

This is similar to a small child who enjoys playing in a plush green yard, soaking up the sunshine and riding their tricycle on the sidewalk. That child is only able to enjoy the benefits of playing in the yard if they are able to respect the boundaries of not running into the road where they could experience immense pain and harm. Playing outside is a wonderful opportunity – but only if done so within the safe boundaries given by adults who know how to protect the child.

Thoughts and emotions that are not controlled and brought under subjection to the truth in God's Word turn into weapons in the hands of the enemy to deceive and ultimately destroy us. What was intended as a gift can quickly become a curse without the oversight of Truth.

WHAT IS THE TRUTH?

Strangely, truth has become a fluid term with multiple definitions. Nowadays, everyone has their "own truth." Unfortunately (and I know modern culture will hate this), that's just not how it works. Truth is truth and you cannot pick and choose "your own."

You can feel a certain way, you can believe something, you can have a certain opinion – but not all of those things can be the truth. Truth is not fluid. There can certainly be some truths that we do not comprehend or understand, but the definition of truth is that it is exact.

You can believe that 2 + 2 = 5 all your life and to learn otherwise could shake the very core of everything you thought was right. But that doesn't change the truth. The truth is, 2 + 2 = 5 is wrong and if you continue in life with this incorrect foundation, you'll end up making a lot of mistakes and going through life wondering why the numbers never add up for you.

Truth is the standard of what is correct and incorrect. It is the revelation of what works and doesn't work. It is the knowledge of what is real versus what is perceived. Only the creator of the universe can establish truth. God is the only one who fully knows, understands and thus is able to communicate truth.

Whatever else anyone might believe – if it contradicts with what God has established as truth – then the belief is an untruth and will not yield the results that are desired. Truth, by definition, cannot be redefined.

THE ATTACK ON TRUTH

"The truth will set you free" (Jn. 8:32). So in order for the enemy to have any chance of destroying you, he first has to uproot the truth. It is Satan's function to "deceive the whole world" (Rev 12:9) and we see this so prevalently in society today. Truth is whatever anyone wants it to be.

In a more extreme example, in the last several years there have been increasingly more advocacy groups[1] fighting for an individual's right to pursue a sexual relationship with children as young as five due to "age fluidity." So a 45-year-old man can say that his "truth" is that he is a 5-year-old girl and therefore he should be allowed to pursue a relationship with a 5-year-old boy regardless of the truth that he is actually a 45-year-old man.

This logic may seem far-fetched now, but the more we push to redefine truth in our society, the wider we open Pandora's box. We live in such an acceptance-driven culture, that untruth has become widely accepted as someone's truth and if you can't accept their truth then you are labeled as being hateful and a bigot. But there is a stark difference between caring about someone and allowing them to change the definition of what is true.

LOVE VS. TRUTH

God loves everyone as they are. He "demonstrates His own love toward us, in that while we were still sinners, Christ died for us" (Rom. 5:8). This is one of my (Robert) favorite verses because it shows us that even while we were still sinners, in our absolute worst condition, God still loved and valued us. God didn't require anyone to live according to His "rules" or to believe the truth before He loved us. He cares about the person who rejects Him entirely and lives according to their own truth as much as He cares about the person who seems to follow all the religious regulations.

Likewise, as the church, we can and should genuinely love everyone - regardless of what they believe. But love doesn't mean redefining the truth. Our witness has to be a strong balance of love and truth. When we get out of alignment of that balance we, as the church, are ineffective.

People must absolutely know how much God loves them. Without understanding how valuable and loved they are, people will see any "truth" that is preached as an effort to fit them into a mold rather than an effort to help them find freedom.

But without truth being preached at all, people will feel loved but they will also stay in their bondages and live a miserable life - never getting to experience the freedom that comes from the truth. In fact, it's *because* we care about people that we become more passionate about establishing truth in their life.

If my child believes he can fly, that doesn't make it true. The truth is, he cannot fly and if he were to jump off a tall building, he would fall and the results would be catastrophic. The truth cannot be redefined no matter how much he feels it or wants to believe it.

I still love him and care about him and fully accept him as my son – but accepting him does not mean that I decide to establish his ability to fly as a new truth. I do not need to accept his incorrect perception that he can fly in order to accept him as my son or love him.

Quite the contrary! Because he believes something that is not true, I care for him all the more - the more I do whatever I can to teach him that he cannot actually fly. Because I know the truth and I know that if he continues to believe an untruth, it will eventually lead to immeasurable pain or even his death. Because I love him, because I care about him and because he is my son, it is all the more reason for me to be more adamant with him regarding the truth.

The exact opposite is happening in the church. We preach God's love, grace and acceptance and then we stop. We don't want to offend anyone so we only reveal the truth that doesn't offend anyone else's "truth."

This leaves us with too many churches filled with defeated Christians trying to walk in their own "truth" who are never able to live the empowered or abundant life that Jesus provides (Jn. 10:10). This happens because the people who are responsible for their growth don't actually love them enough to tell them *the* truth. We have too many Christians who fear man more than they fear God and won't speak *the* truth because it might offend *their* truth. But that isn't love, it's self-preservation!

Furthermore, anyone who knows the way to an abundant life and withholds it from someone, doesn't truly love them. I don't think anyone who witnesses a person watch as their loved one jumps off a building believing they could fly would say that they really cared about that person. Love is not openly accepting everyone's truth without question. Love is showing compassion towards people and having a desire for them to live abundantly - even if the process requires correcting their untruth.

When we talk about the permanency of truth, understand that we are not preaching a message of rejection or superiority. We are preaching a message of love. Because there is no reason for the children of God to live in such defeat when His promises of life, joy and peace are so readily available to those who know the truth and apply it.

It is a sad deception of the enemy when people believe they will find joy if they can break free from the expectations placed on them by others and simply be fully allowed to "live their truth." The irony is that the temporary feeling of freedom found in living their truth unhindered will always be followed by a wake of pain to others and eventual pain to themselves. And although most people have to walk out that process themselves in order to fully realize the truth in these words, the good news is that you don't have to suffer through years of trial and error to find freedom.

CHOOSE TRUTH

At this point, we've established that there is only one truth. That truth is found in the Word of God. Which means that any thoughts or emotions that lead you to believe something that is contrary to the Word of God, is not the truth. It is a lie.

If a feeling or thought is a lie, that lends us to conclude that you can choose which thoughts and feelings you keep and which ones you reject. You have a choice. That doesn't mean the process of choosing the right thoughts and emotions doesn't take effort – we'll get into what that process looks like in subsequent chapters - but for now, you must first understand that you can choose your thoughts and emotions.

How you feel is not who you are. What you think is not who you are. You do not have to follow every emotion that you feel. You do not have to follow every thought that comes into your mind. Your emotions and thoughts are subject to a higher power and if you are a Christian, that higher power resides inside of you and the higher power that resides inside of you has the potential to direct your thoughts and emotions into what is true.

Truth in your Identity

God did not make a mistake when He "formed you in the womb" (Jr. 1:5). We live in a fallen world and with that comes the biological consequences of imperfections, but any abnormalities in your biological make-up does not change your worth in God's eyes nor does it change His ability to love you, accept you and fulfill you. God declares that you are "awesomely and wonderfully made" (Ps. 139:14) just the way He created you in the womb – without any further altercation, enhancements or adjustment.

Furthermore, since God is not bound to or surprised by the unfolding of events in the scope of time, any flaws that you may have or think you are able to identify within yourself were already accounted for in God's eyes and He already formed your days for you accordingly (Ps. 139:16). Meaning, God has already made arrangements to cover whatever excuse or justification that you can offer Him as a reason that you do not have value or an excuse as to why you cannot follow Him in obedience. Your identity is in Christ and in nothing else. It is only in following your identity in Christ that you can realize who you really are regardless of who you think you might be outside of God's truth.

It's easy to count yourself out when it comes to believing that you can live a truly fulfilled and purposed life as a child of God. There may be one-hundred options that you cannot pursue in life because of your flaws, but God is able to provide the one option that matters. The way to find that one option is to first believe that you have worth and that your identity is in God and not in anything that this physical world can establish for you. Secondly, believe that God knows "'the plans that I have for you,' declares the Lord, 'plans for prosperity and not for disaster, to give you a future and a hope" (Jr. 29:11).

As you put those beliefs into action, and move forward in your life with perseverance (not quitting too soon) and obedience to God, He will open doors and provide opportunities for you to discover who He is more profoundly and who you are in Him. These revelations will ultimately bring deep fulfillment to your life.

We must emphasize that this only works if you understand the truth, believe the truth and walk in obedience to the truth. Sometimes the results of this process come quickly, but the majority of the time the results only become evident through perseverance - continually identifying the lies and declaring the truth over your identity. As you continue through those trials, you will grow in perseverance and when perseverance has its full effect, you will be "perfect and complete, lacking in nothing" (Jm. 1:4).

Truth in your Mind

Two of the fruits of the Spirit are joy and peace (Gal. 5:22). Galatians further outlines that these two traits, along with other desirable emotions are only available as we walk in the Spirit. When we walk according to our flesh, we don't get to experience the fruits of walking in the Spirit. There may be temporary moments of happiness or the outwardly appearance of good fruit, but the permanent residence of these things does not take place unless we have fully submitted our lives to God.

If Jesus is "the way, and the truth, and the life" (Jn. 14:6) and Satan is the "ruler of this world" (Jn. 14:30) and "he is a liar and the father of lies" (Jn. 8:44), then it stands to reason that if we believe the lies of the enemy and live our lives according to that belief (i.e. "walk in the flesh") then we will experience the opposite of joy and peace. And what's the opposite of joy and peace?

If you guessed anxiety and depression, I think that's a pretty good guess. So if we begin to believe the lies more than we believe God's Truth, then spiritually-speaking, it makes complete sense why so many of us would be struggling through anxiety and depression. Our culture tries to categorize these kinds of struggles as purely "mental health" issues. But since we are a Spirit and we have a soul and live in a body (more on this in the next chapter), it's not just our "mental" health that's struggling, it's really our "spiritual" health that is struggling.

When we entertain the deceitful thoughts that enter our minds regularly and believe that every time we *feel* sad it must mean that we *are* sad, we are allowing our thoughts and our feelings to dictate what truth is to us. This walking in the flesh ultimately leads to the lack of joy and peace – which our culture would identify as depression and anxiety.

If your mind starts to get carried away with all the "what ifs" of every decision or possible scenario that you could find yourself in and you don't ever stop those lies and declare the truth instead, then you will find yourself anxious.

These negative emotions activate the beta-endorphin and dopamine pathways - the reward center of the brain that is also associated with substance addictions.[2] If we continually fail to regulate our thoughts and emotions, then we can become addicted to the negative emotion. And like most addictions, as your body becomes more tolerant of the substance, it will need higher levels of that substance to reach the same levels of satisfaction.[3]

It's important to note that this kind of emotional addiction doesn't happen simply because someone was born with a chemical imbalance. It is our brain's response to the emotions and thoughts we choose to keep and which ones we choose to reject – a process known as neuroplasticity.[4]

The same is true for depression. It's OK to feel sad about a situation or feel regret over a mistake. Those emotions are in place to help us know when we need to grow in ourselves and in our relationship with God. What is not OK is when those normal sad emotions are left without the application of God's Truth and over time, what is "normal" can spiral into suicidal depression.

Gloria's Story

There was about a two-year period in my life that I (Gloria) battled with depression. It started off as a collection of fairly normal disappointing days that were left unregulated and eventually snowballed into an inability to get out of bed, non-stop feelings of hopelessness and a belief that I had no value in the world or in my family and I began entertaining suicidal thoughts and plans on a daily basis for the last couple months of that season.

I had nothing circumstantially to be depressed about – I wanted for nothing, had a great family and a promising future – but this only served to make my depression worse because there was nothing "wrong" and yet I was still depressed and so there was nothing I could change in my circumstances to be happier. This didn't stop me from trying to place blame on stresses outside of my control. For a little while, I tried to blame everything or everyone that wasn't perfect. But eventually I had to come to terms that it wasn't my circumstances, it was just me.

I knew that my depression was holding my family back from being able to "live life abundantly" and I knew that they loved me too much to move on with life without me if I were still alive. So my thought process was that if I removed myself from their lives, then they would be free to find someone else who could be the person that they truly deserved – and by NOT committing suicide I was being selfish and putting my own desire to exist above my family's best interest. Of course, this was all a lie and writing it out several years later I can see how deceived I was. But during that time, it made perfect sense to me.

I tried to "think myself happy" and failed nearly every time. I tried forcing myself to get up and "do one productive thing." I tried cutting off social media. I tried working out. I tried eating right.

I attempted to worship. I attempted to read my Bible. I prayed constantly. I prayed that God would give me joy and take away my depression. I doubted everything because God promised me freedom, joy and peace and I wasn't experiencing any of it – so I doubted the existence of God, I doubted my salvation. I questioned everything about who I was and what I believed.

I felt like I had tried everything, but there were two things I was not doing – I was not fighting the lies and I wasn't declaring the truth. I was leaning more into God and praying but I was praying for deliverance from something that He had given me the power to control – I just didn't know I could control it and so I didn't try very hard. I don't know if the source of my depression was as simple as sadness that I allowed to grow over time, biological imbalances or if the enemy specifically targeted me from the beginning - or all of the above. But I do know that regardless of the reason it started, the process to getting breakthrough is largely the same – fight the lies, declare the truth.

The truth is that joy is a choice, it is not a temporal feeling. We can "feel" happiness sporadically for many internal or external reasons, but we can "choose" joy. That's why James 1:2 can command us to "consider it all joy" and Philippians 4:4 can instruct us to "rejoice in the Lord always." Because it's something we can choose to do, not something we have to wait to find us.

We choose to have joy when we resist the lie that we don't have any control of how we feel (Jm. 4:7), spend time in God's presence (Ps. 16:11) and think on things that we are thankful for in all circumstances (1 Th. 5:18) with the understanding that every season is temporary and "joy comes in the morning" (Ps. 30:5) if we so choose.

Combatting anxiety is the same process. Resist the lie that the outcome of every situation is exclusively based on your ability to make the right decision when Psalm 37:23 says "the steps of a man are established by the Lord." Resist the lie that tells you that your world is going to fall apart at any moment because Philippians 4:6-7 says "do not be anxious about anything, but in everything by prayer and pleading with thanksgiving let your requests be made known to God. And the peace of God, which surpasses all comprehension, will guard your hearts and minds in Christ Jesus."

Then make special note that this promise states "with thanksgiving". So when you feel paralyzing fear overwhelm you, be obedient to what scripture says and give your requests to God and adjust your thoughts from fear to thoughts of things you are thankful for and an understanding that when you are depending on God, He is leading your steps.

Truth in your Relationships

The core of our lives is made up of the relationships we keep. Whether that's our relationship with God, relationships with our bosses and co-workers, relationships with friends and family or our romantic relationships – these relationships are the building block of our lives. Being able to navigate all these relationships through the lens of truth is essential to the success of our lives overall.

Because we live in such an emotion-based culture, we make decisions regarding our relationships accordingly. If a church leader offends us, we go to a new church. If a family member fails to appreciate us one too many times, we cut them off. If our boss consistently overlooks us, we find a new job. If our spouse no longer makes us happy, we find a new spouse.

These actions don't reflect any standard of truth – they are simply actions taken exclusively based on our feelings. Most of the time, no consideration is given to whether or not God has called us to a specific church - regardless of offense. We seem to forget that God commands us to forgive those who have hurt us unconditionally. We can find ourselves giving very little weight to staying at a job that we know God directed us to when we feel like it's not going anywhere. We easily dismiss the mandate for a marriage to be inseparable and refuse to do whatever it takes to make it work.

Not only should you not be making these life-altering decisions based on your own thoughts and emotions, but those emotions shouldn't even be given weight in determining the "right" decision. Logic and emotions can lead you an entirely opposite direction from where God wants you. If God is on the throne of your life, then God gets to decide – whether according to His Word or according to His Spirit.

I (Robert) was working in a position where I felt overwhelmingly overlooked for years. Unprompted, I was offered an opportunity that would have paid double my salary and given me the respect of a high-level position. Both my intellect and emotion supported this move uncontested. Turning it down would have looked foolish to anyone looking from the outside in.

However, I absolutely knew where God had called me to be and He had not yet released me to move away from where He had last placed me. So I had to go against my thoughts and emotions and make a decision according to God's truth. Years later, God was right. I cannot imagine what direction I would have missed in my life if I had not understood the importance of living according to truth instead of by thoughts and emotions.

Truth in your Marriage

One of the primary areas in which we witness a lack of understanding of truth destroy more lives is through broken marriages. When a marriage is torn apart, it leaves shattered fragments that negatively affect everyone involved. Even if you are reading this and you are not yet married, it's important to understand how uncontrolled emotions and suffocating thoughts can affect your future relationships. This isn't a marriage book so we won't go too far into this, but if this is an area that you are currently struggling in we recommend Gary Thomas's book, "Sacred Marriage." You might also consider our marriage book "CounterCulture Marriage" (shameless plug).

What we do want to emphasize on this topic is that your feelings do not dictate what is true. We have heard many couples end their marriages because "they fell out of love" or they "fell in love with someone else." In our culture, marriage has become a union that exists to make two individuals happy and when that happiness decreases, the reasoning to continue in a marriage also decrease. But marriage is a commitment, not an experience. Every marriage will go through seasons of loving emotions and seasons where they feel completely disconnected from their spouse. But it's in continuing to grow towards each other despite the lack of positive emotions that causes you to more deeply feel the loving emotions when they do circle back around.

How the world defines "love" is not the way God defines "love". According to 1 Corinthians 13:4-7, "love is patient, love is kind, it is not jealous; love does not brag, it is not arrogant. It does not act disgracefully, it does not seek its own benefit; it is not provoked, does not keep an account of a wrong suffered, it does not rejoice in unrighteousness, but rejoices with the truth; it keeps every confidence, it believes all things, hopes all things, endures all things." We've heard this verse recited so many times that it's easy to gloss over it. But we encourage you to read again and apply it to yourself to determine whether you are actually operating out of love or selfishness.

Just like joy, love is also not an emotion. Love is a command (Jn. 15:12). It's not something we can fall out of or fall into. It's something we proactively and intentionally do. Gary Thomas says, "in culture, love is expressed as a passive activity, something that happens to us. But in Christian love, we choose where to place our affection." To declare you love someone is to declare that you are going to place someone else's well-being ahead of your own. The romantic feelings that most people associate with "love" in our culture is not love, but infatuation.

When someone says they "fell in love with someone else", they are being led by their emotions and have allowed those emotions to lead them to invest their time and energy into someone who was not their spouse and that resulted in a connection that they now associate with a positive feeling. And if that spouse believes that their emotions dictate what is truth in their life without submitting that emotion to God's truth, then they will actually believe that they "fell in love with someone else."

The truth is, they chose to fall in love with someone else. And when you understand that your thoughts and emotions are not in charge then when someone else sparks your interest, you can take that emotion or thought captive and make it obedient to Christ (2 Co. 10:5) by setting up safeguards in regards to that disobedient relationship and being more intentional about investing in your spouse.

This doesn't mean that you will feel romantic love towards your spouse instantly once you make the decision to act according to truth instead of your emotions. Especially if you've created a soul tie with someone who is not your spouse or you've been betrayed, it takes time and consistent intentionality to force your emotions back towards your spouse. The Infidelity Recovery Institute states best case scenario for recovery is 18-months.[5] But when compared to a lifelong marriage spanning decades, a few years of working against your emotions in order to save your marriage is a small price to pay. Your only other alternative is to divorce, start over and circle around the same mountain of being emotionally-led and getting divorced again or eventually learn how to control your emotions and sacrifice those few years of intentionality anyway.

You are in charge of your emotions. If you want your emotions to be positive towards your spouse, then start selflessly investing in your spouse and seek to understand the truth in regards to your marriage and areas where you can grow. Choosing to focus on the admirable qualities of your spouse instead of dwelling on the negatives is scriptural (Pp. 4:8) and can go a long way here. The cultural advice that tells you to "follow your heart" is advice that doesn't take into account that your heart doesn't know truth and in fact scripture says "the heart is more deceitful than all else and is desperately sick; who can understand it?" (Jr. 17:9)

FREEDOM IN THE TRUTH

In order to have victory in all these areas of our lives we must first know the truth. It's nearly impossible to get your head above the water when you don't know which way is up. God's Word is the truth. Any emotions or thoughts that contradict God's Word is a lie – no matter how real it may feel.

We must continually remind ourselves that no matter how real something feels or how logical something seems, that God's ways are higher than our ways and His thoughts are higher than our thoughts (Is. 55:9). Any belief that places man's intellect above the intellect of the God who created all things is foolishness.

Once we've established in our own belief system that the standard of truth in our lives is who God says we are and what God says we can do, then we can move forward.

"ANY BELIEF THAT PLACES MAN'S INTELLECT ABOVE THE INTELLECT OF THE GOD WHO CREATED ALL THINGS IS FOOLISHNESS.

\\ 3
WHO
YOU ARE

"Now may the God of peace Himself sanctify you entirely;
and may your spirit and soul and body be kept complete..."
1 Thessalonians 5:23a

In order to understand how you can take control of your emotions and thoughts, you first have to understand who you are. You consist of three parts: "spirit and soul and body…" (I Th. 5:23) just as God is made up of three parts, "the Father and the Son and of the Holy Spirit" (Mt. 28:19) and He "created man in His own image" (Gn. 1:27).

You are a spirit, you live in a body and you have a soul. Your spirit is what makes you a living creature, your body is your biological make-up and your soul consists of your mind, will and emotions.

In a world that does not acknowledge the existence of God, people dismiss their life-giving spirit and assume that their soul is who they are - which explains why people believe that their thoughts and emotions are what give them life. When we consider that our soul is not what gives us life - but it is our spirit - then we can more fully understand that our thoughts and emotions are not who we are and they can be redirected by our spirits.

No part of the three components of your being operate independently of the other. Every part is deeply entangled with the other parts and every part can cause changes in each of the other parts.

YOUR BODY

Your body is your biological being. It's your skin, your organs, your blood, the neurons in your brain, the various chemicals that are produced.

It's the sweaty palms when you are nervous, the headache that you get when you are stressed, the tears that flow from your eyes when you are grieving, the hormones that rage when you are sexually stimulated - bodily functions easily measured by science.

Most of the time, these measurable biological responses are triggered by a thought that materializes into an emotion that manifests itself biologically. There are chemical and hormonal imbalances that can exist in our bodies apart from emotional triggers. However, although your current biological makeup may determine where you are starting from, it is not the exclusive indicator of where you can end up.

Scientifically-speaking, your chemical imbalances can influence your thoughts and emotions, but as Dr. L.M. Garća-Segura states in his abstract on "Hormones and Brain Plasticity," your "brain plasticity [also] plays an essential role in the regulation of hormonal levels."[1] It can go both ways and as Jurie Rossouw states in his article "How Neuroplasticity Changes the Brain," "we can purposefully change our neural organization through directed effort."[2] So although it plays a role, we are not actually as helplessly subject to our biological makeup as many in our popular culture would like to believe.

Likewise, from a spiritual perspective, what happens in our bodies is triggered by something that is happening in our souls. Our body's physical reaction to stimuli is not the determining factor for what *is* true but rather the biological reaction to what we *believe* to be true – which may or may not *actually* be true.

For example, it would be an incorrect assumption to think that you are "in love" with someone *because* your palms get sweaty and you get butterflies when you are around them. A more accurate assessment would be that there is an emotional attraction exclusively in your soul (mind, will and emotions) that is causing your body to react in such a way. But if you reverse the causation between those two elements, then you allow your body's natural chemical nuances to dictate what you believe to be true and it becomes a self-fulfilling prophecy.

This is also true with your thoughts. If you learn that you have a legitimate mild chemical imbalance that causes you to feel depressed and you adopt that diagnosis as an unchangeable truth, you are far more likely not to regulate your negative thoughts because "that's just who you are." Subsequently those negative thoughts become habitual – even more so if you vocalize your negativity.[3] Those habitual negative thoughts "forge pathways in the brain" (MindHealth360)[4] and cause more stress hormones to be released and over time cause a more severe imbalance than what you started with – a self-fulfilling prophecy.

You may not have had a severe imbalance to begin with, but because the truth was determined by your biological state instead of the truth of God's Word in your Spirit, that truth became a belief in your soul and further informed your body to solidify that belief.

1 Corinthians 6:18 says "whoever sins sexually, sins against their own body." This specifically addresses sex, but it gives us a clear understanding that what your soul initiates you to do with your body has spiritual implications. It's all connected. You cannot do something exclusively with your body and it not affect the most intimate part of yourself - your spirit. You cannot feel or think something in your soul that doesn't affect your body and so on.

YOUR SOUL

Your soul is made up of your mind, will and emotions. Although the Bible does not explicitly state this, we can gather from a collection of scriptural references that those three elements are what comprise the soul.

In Job 6:7, Job references his will when he says "my soul refuses to touch them; they are like loathsome food to me." Then in Job 10:1, he references his emotions when he states "I am disgusted with my own life; I will express my complaint freely; I will speak in the bitterness of my soul." A Psalmist references his mind in Psalm 94:19 when he declares, "when my anxious thoughts multiply within me, Your comfort delights my soul."

The soul can operate independently of your Spirit but in doing so, will wreak havoc on your physical body. Although our brain and neuron connections are part of our physical body, the thoughts created by those connections are our soul. Our soul desires to do things, feels things and thinks about things.

Our soul is not who we are, but it is what makes us a unique individual - it is how we feel, how we respond to critiques or compliments, and encompasses our personal desires and motives. Our soul is also not unchanging. Just like our physical body changes, so does our soul. This contradicts popular statements like "be who you are" and "this is who I am, I can't change it". The truth is, you can change. That doesn't mean changing is easy or doesn't feel unnatural for a season - but combined with the strength of our spirit – eventually our soul can do a complete 180 and it will feel completely natural.

YOUR SPIRIT

It is our spirit that gives us life. Because we are made in the image of God, our spirits have eternal life. But it is only when we are connected with God's Spirit that we can have eternal life in Heaven.

Pre-salvation, your spirit is corrupted by sin and is helplessly controlled by your soul. There is no power in your spirit apart from God's Spirit – in effect, your spirit is "dead."

When you are saved, God's Spirit joins with your spirit and a new creation is formed. This is what it means to be "born again." "It is the Spirit that gives [spiritual] life" (Jn. 6:63) and once God's Spirit lives within you, all the power and authority that exists in God's Spirit now exists within your spirit – including the power to control your soul.

Your spirit is now Holy, acceptable, forgiven and perfect before God. You may wonder - if you are holy, forgiven and perfect - why don't you think or feel it? That is exactly the juxtaposition that led to this book.

Your Spirit has been saved, your soul is being saved and your body will be saved (when we receive our glorified bodies). Therefore, even though you ARE saved, you will not always think like it or feel it – because those things are based in your soul.

There may be moments you don't believe you are who God says you are or moments you mess up. In those times, you do not need to question your salvation, you need to remind yourself that those are areas of your soul - your mind, will and emotions - that need to be renewed. That renewal process is call sanctification and it is indeed, a process. A process that takes time and intentionality and continues for the span of our earthly lives.

DOG METAPHOR

In order to give you a visual of how this works, we're going to borrow a slightly adjusted metaphor from Chapter 11: Lust vs. Love of our book, "CounterCulture Marriage." This is not a foolproof metaphor but it can give you a good representation of the dynamics at play:

Think of yourself as a person walking a dog on a leash. Your soul is the dog, your spirit is the dog-walker and your physical body is the leash that connects both dog and dog-walker into a single unit.

As you take your dog (soul) for a walk in the world, the dog is confronted with many stimuli. It's natural for your dog to get a whiff of something in the air and take notice, see a squirrel and want to immediately go chase it or smell another dog and innately become aggressive if it's the same sex or be uncontrollably attracted if it's a dog of the opposite sex (especially if they are in heat). Sometimes your dog is distracted by the world around him, sometimes there's an aggressor provoking him and sometimes the dog just has ideas and a mind of his own.

But no matter the stimuli or distraction, if the dog is on a leash and the dog-walker is in firm control, it doesn't take much to yank the dog back on the right path and refocused on where he should be going. The dog-walker is in control and what it produces is a beautiful and peaceful walk through the park with both dog-walker and dog arriving at the intended destination.

That's the ideal scenario. Unfortunately, what is far more common to see in our world - metaphorically speaking - is a 250lb saint bernard running rampant in the streets attached to a leash that is dragging behind it either a dead dog-walker (non-Christian) or a terribly weak and feeble dog-walker (weak Christian) that is helplessly stumbling after the dog.

This creates a situation where we have a dog that is wreaking havoc on the streets chasing down every whiff in the air, overreacting in fear to every trash can clanking together and/or relieving itself in the middle of sidewalks for others to accidentally step in. A loose, out-of-control dog is bad enough, but this dog is also dragging a leash and a person on the other end, which multiplies the wreckage exponentially.

This is what our life is like when our soul - our mind, will and emotions - are in total control and our spirits are too weak to mandate otherwise. Every decision we make is based on our emotional response (ignited by a thought), and our body quickly aligns itself with our soul as it's dragged through the mud and our spirits – the only part of us that has the truth – is helplessly dragged behind.

Remember, that in our example, the dog, the leash and the dog-walker are permanently attached to each other – just as our body, soul and spirit have no choice but to co-exist until our body dies. So simply letting go of the leash is not a viable option. The only way for the dog-walker (our spirit) to gain control of the dog (our soul) is to become stronger than the dog. The leash, representing our body, will always fall into alignment with and function in support of whichever party is in control – whether that means we are dragging our bodies through the mud or our bodies are being kept clean and being used for a purpose.

This is a prime visual for the statement, "strengthening your spirit and starving your flesh" in relation to becoming a more mature believer. The "flesh" in this context is not necessarily exclusively your physical body, but your inner man (the untransformed parts of your soul and your body) that has to constantly be put into subjection to the Spirit.

If you are living a life where "you present your bodies a living sacrifice, holy, acceptable to God" (Rm. 12:1), then metaphorically speaking, you are a 250lb bodybuilder walking a 5lb toy poodle. It doesn't matter how distracted that toy poodle may get or how much it may have the urge to chase after something; you - as the bodybuilder - would not have any issues keeping your toy poodle in line. That doesn't mean that the toy poodle doesn't get urges - it does, but it is on a leash that is being controlled by a bodybuilder; therefore, everything is in alignment.

THE PROCESS IS WORTH IT

Keeping with the dog metaphor - in order to not be controlled by our thoughts and emotions, we need to build ourselves as stronger, weightier dog-walkers and reduce our dogs to that of a tiny toy breed variety. This gives us the luxury of still owning a dog and enjoying all the benefits of dog ownership without destroying our entire worlds.

Strengthening our spirits and weakening our flesh is a process that we'll dive into in more detail in the last chapters of this book. But it is a process that takes intentionality and effort. You wouldn't expect to see any significant results in your body after only working out for a few days. Likewise, the process to strengthening your spirit also takes consistency and longevity.

It's absolutely not the path of least resistance. In fact, in addition to our own desires, there is also an evil force that constantly "prowls around like a roaring lion, seeking someone to devour" (1 Pt. 5:8). In order to achieve victory, you are going to be constantly fighting against yourself and a very real enemy. You will have to have a determination in you that wants the victory bad enough that it motivates you to keep pushing forward.

Perhaps the thought of going through an uphill process seems like a lot of work and you are saying to yourself, "I just want to live free and happy. I want to be the dog living in the wild, free to do my own thing." The problem is, that doesn't exist. Sure, if you are a dog without a leash or perhaps just a short leash, then perhaps you could run wild and be happy. But you're not just the dog. You're also the leash and the walker - you're a three-fold being. So even if you are allowed to chase after every rabbit "freely," you may find some fleeting happiness in the moment, but you're still attached to the dead person on the other end and that dead person is your spirit – the core of who you are. So even after your "dog" has caught all the wild rabbits that your little heart desires – you're still dead inside and that death is an eternal death. Any freedom is only perceived, not true freedom.

True freedom ultimately leads to life. When we choose to have a genuine relationship with a loving God - who we allow to develop us and lead us into the purpose we are created for – that's when we are truly "happy" and "free" from the things that control us.

"NATURAL" DOESN'T EQUAL "RIGHT"

Just because something is "natural" or "normal" doesn't mean it's "acceptable" in God's eyes. Our flesh will always gravitate towards what's natural, but the Spirit gravitates towards what is holy.

A non-believer may feel empty inside, but a believer who lives in between the pull of the flesh and the pull of the Spirit will always feel the defeat of the constant struggle. It's only when we completely give ourselves exclusively to our flesh or our Spirit that we can be released from the struggle.

Giving ourselves over to the flesh will release the struggle temporarily but will ultimately lead to destruction. Giving ourselves over to the Spirit will feel like a death temporarily, but will ultimately lead to life and peace. We don't just mean life eternally but life abundantly on earth as well. Romans 8:6 says "for the mind set on the flesh is death, but the mind set on the Spirit is life and peace.

As a simplified example: When a couple gets married, that marriage doesn't automatically eliminate every attraction to someone who is not their spouse. Those attractions would be considered "natural" and "normal." We have eyes, we have preferences and we are still able to form emotional connections to people. Being in a marital union doesn't take away those natural charges.

However, if we have committed to living our life according to the Truth in God's Word, then we have to choose to turn away from any potential extra-marital connections and choose to invest in our connection with our spouse in order to fulfill our marital commitment. This act of sacrificing a desire that we would typically "naturally" pursue in order to submit ourselves in obedience to God's Word will feel like the death of our fleshly desires. Because it is. Jesus said "If anyone wishes to come after Me, he must deny himself, take up his cross and follow Me" (Mk. 8:34). Galatians 5:24 states that "those who belong to Christ Jesus crucified the flesh with its passions and desires."

Ultimately, the death of our flesh is what gives us the opportunity to have a deeper and fuller marriage union, positions us to be able to receive God's promise in our lives and frees our marriage to be a productive part of changing the world for the better.

Whereas succumbing to our "natural" desires in entertaining a connection with someone who is not our spouse will ultimately lead to destruction. This destruction will occur in the natural with the separation of a marriage and even more destruction in the lives of children.

The destruction will also happen in our spirit because it will cause distraction, shame and a struggle in our relationship with God. It will cause destruction in our maturity because we fail to grow in perseverance and self-control - character traits that are necessary for us to remain steadfast in our calling on this earth as virtuous (i.e. strong) individuals.

The emotional benefits available in pursuing the extramarital relationship are temporary at best. As long as an understanding of the Truth has yet to be realized and the necessary character traits fail to be developed, then it's likely that the destructive cycle will happen again several times throughout an individual's life.

This ultimately leads to a life that is consumed by "following ones' heart" and subsequently, a life spent managing the consequences of our heart's choices rather than a life dedicated to serving those we are called to and bearing eternal fruit. And so, doing only what is "natural" without submitting to Truth becomes the destruction of the potential fruit from a life well-lived as well.

We are not denying that the extramarital relationship was "natural." We are saying that during seasons of discovery and growth, we have to daily choose obedience over what is "natural" in order to realize the benefits of obedience. As we continue in pursuit of God, what was exclusively "obedience" becomes our new "natural" in that specific area of our lives unless we choose to return to our fleshly patterns.

James 1:4 states "let endurance have its perfect result, so that you may be perfect and complete, lacking in nothing." Meaning, it's only when we practice the art of staying steadfast in our pursuit of God, daily renewing our minds and setting our eyes on Jesus and turning away from our "natural desires" that we can bear lasting fruit on this earth. Any other strategy will yield temporary results or a lifetime of heartache.

This example was specifically for married couples, but apply this same idea to issues surrounding your identity, your mental health and your relationships. It may feel "natural" for you to be attracted to someone of the same sex, "natural" to feel melancholy or anxious or "natural" to walk away from a relationship or position God has placed you in so you can pursue something totally different. These things may very well be "natural" for you, but if they reside outside of God's will according to scripture then those "natural" feelings will ultimately lead you to brokenness in the long run.

We choose to turn towards holiness despite what's "natural." We choose to be obedient despite what we feel or what thoughts occur in our minds. And it's in that obedience that God Himself reveals His love to us more fully and more intensely than any temporary satisfaction we could have gained from superficial "natural" pursuits.

„WE MUST CHOOSE TO TURN TOWARDS HOLINESS DESPITE WHAT'S "NATURAL."

\\ 4
SELF-CONTROL
FREAK

*"Like a city that is broken into and without walls so is a
person who has no self-control over his spirit."*

Proverbs 25:28

Learning how to live a life based on Truth rather than your thoughts and emotions can be handled a few different ways depending on the source of your troubles. There could be biological imbalances, spiritual attacks, incorrect belief systems and/or a lack of self-control at play in your life.

THE BIOLOGICAL COMPONENT

In our natural bodies, people can experience chemical imbalances to such an extreme level that it makes it impossible to have victory in their thoughts and emotions. Sometimes, this kind of extreme situation requires medication that is temporarily necessary for a person to be able to have the mental clarity to even start the process to more permanent healing.

Then there may be the smallest fraction of mankind that suffer from permanent imbalances and disabilities that would serve as the exception to what we discuss in this book and can only be helped through permanent medications. However, it needs to be understood that this is the rare minority of situations. Our culture has so popularized these medical diagnoses that it has kept the majority of people in bondage who otherwise could have found victory if they were forced to push through without the convenient crutch of a now socially-accepted label.

This may sound harsh, but hear our hearts. We, in no way, want to shame the small percentage of the population who have legitimate biological obstacles to overcome. However, we also need to acknowledge that almost every person reading this book most likely does not fall into this "biological" category and is able to find victory through a deeper understanding of the obstacles in their minds and hearts.

THE SPIRITUAL COMPONENT

When considering our existence on a physical earth with unsanctified souls largely influenced by the spiritual realm, it is a foolish world we live in that diminishes the potential effects of demonic forces. There are people who are legitimately battling spiritual beings that torment their minds and render them seemingly powerless in having victory in their lives.

These bondages are next-level and can originate through things like unforgiveness and unhealed trauma or be passed down through generations. Identifying the source of these bondages and oppressions and unpacking them in a way that can lead you to healing requires more than what is communicated in this book.

If you feel it's possible that this is the source of your troubles, we encourage you to read Neil T. Anderson's "The Bondage Breaker"[1] and find a licensed Christian professional who has a firm understand of the spiritual elements at play.

THE BELIEF COMPONENT

Without the proper belief system, people can be doomed to failure simply because they don't know that any other way of life exists. Hosea 4:6 says "my people are destroyed for lack of knowledge." If an individual is never taught that all their decisions should be based on God's Word instead of their feelings and thoughts, then what is to be expected than a generation of people who sense no obligation to adhere to Truth and service to God but rather live according to their own selfish emotions and are carried away wherever their thoughts lead them?

This applies to non-Christians and Christians alike. That is why God commanded us to "go, therefore, and make disciples" (Mt. 28:19). Christians without discipleship may be saved but live the same lives as their non-Christian counterparts because they don't have any greater knowledge of the Truth and only know what the world teaches them. So who is to blame except the people who God appointed to disciple His people?

In our current culture, the majority of believers and non-believers both make decisions regarding who they marry, why they get divorced, what jobs they take or quit, how they handle their finances, what church they attend or leave, what family members they disown, how they honor (or dishonor) authority, etc., based on how they feel and their own opinions rather than submitting to God's instructions. And this always ultimately leads to pain and destruction.

Even as young children, we are asked "what do you want to be when you grow up?" and then told that "you can be anything you want to be." Although we understand that these statements are intended to instill a sense of vision and confidence in a young child, it can also instill a sense of pride and selfishness – "I" can do anything - even if it's apart from God - or *only* what "I" want to do matters and that's what I should be focused on.

But how many parents ask their children what God wants them to do when they grow-up or tell them that they can accomplish anything that God calls them to accomplish because God is their source and not themselves? Those questions position children at a young age that their lives are not their own and their decisions are not their own but that everything in their mind, will and emotions must come under submission to God.

These things shouldn't be taught out of legalism or religion but out of a sincere belief in the Bible and an understanding that the promises of God are available to us as long as we follow the instructions. These promises come from a God who created us and knows exactly what each individual needs to be fully fulfilled in life – a fulfillment that can only come from having an intimate relationship with our Creator.

Such thinking seems archaic in our modern world where the fight for freedom - unconfined by any theologies, moralities, opinions or science - runs rampant. But those who fight for those apparent freedoms end up only in a cycle of defeat as they learn over a lifetime that no amount of perceived freedom ever truly brings true freedom without submission to the Creator.

"People are slaves to whatever has mastered them" (2 Pt. 2:19). "Everyone who sins is a slave to sin" (Jn. 8:34) and only "Christ has set us free" (Ga. 5:1). You ultimately have a choice: live a life in misery with temporary wins fighting for your "freedoms" or submit your life to Christ and relinquish your perceived freedoms in order to be who God created you to be and experience spiritual freedom from the inside out.

God desires to have an active and vibrant relationship with His children but the world – and the church - needs the people who understand these truths to teach them in their circles of influence. Otherwise, the truth exists but is rendered ineffective because it is not applied. In order to apply the truth, we come across a topic that has left many informed Christians still struggling - self-control.

THE SELF-CONTROL COMPONENT

This is a word you don't hear glorified too often. People may reference it as a positive trait but then when asked to apply it to their behaviors, emotions or thoughts, it's quickly dismissed as something that hinders an individual from truly being themselves.

Most likely, you are not part of the fraction of the population that suffers from an incurable disability that causes unchangeable chemical imbalances and most likely, you are not tormented by a possessing evil spirit. And if you bought this book, it's highly likely that you already have a belief system that understands the benefits and importance of surrendering your life and decisions to God.

Then this is where the vast majority of us fall short – we are a people that need to strengthen our self-control muscles within our mind, will and emotions.

A CITY WITH NO WALLS

Proverbs 25:28 says that "like a city whose walls are broken through is a person who lacks self-control."

When we think of a city, we think of an area bursting at the seams with people, ideas, talents, productivity, creativity, relationships, activities, etc. There is so much life and potential contained inside a city. That's not much unlike how God created you. You have skills, talents, ideas and above all else a purpose and a calling that God specifically designed you for. You are a life full of potential. A "city" of activity within yourself.

The walls of a city are built to protect everything within those walls from outside enemy attacks. It doesn't matter how valuable or how much potential a city contains, if an enemy attacks and there is no protection of the walls, everything within the city is destroyed. And all that could have been used for good is then wasted for the enemy's pleasures and purpose.

Ask yourself if your life is without the walls of self-control. Without the walls of self-control, any wayward thoughts, fleeting emotions, person or circumstance that provokes you will destroy your life and all the potential that your life could be is never seen.

What a devastating depiction of what a lack of self-control produces. And yet, with the sharp increases in depression, anxiety, obesity, infidelity, suicides and divorces, it's clear that what we lack is self-control. We are not implying that all issues can be overcome by simply exhibiting some self-control - that grossly minimizes the severity of your struggles. However, it is important to recognize that if you're going to find victory, it's going to take the supernatural power of the Holy Spirit growing and developing you. Complete victory is the fruit of your ability to practice self-control partnered with God's ability to heal and transform you internally.

BUILDING YOUR SELF-CONTROL MUSCLES

If you wanted to build your arm muscles, you'd go to the gym and start lifting weights. You wouldn't expect immediate results that first day or the second day – but you'd understand that building noticeable muscles takes consistency and commitment to the training. You also wouldn't expect to go in and be able to lift 250lbs if you've never lifted weights before.

Likewise, self-control is like a muscle and that muscle has to be trained and strengthened. As you start out on this journey of building your walls of self-control, don't be discouraged if you just "can't" do it. You can do it, but don't start out with the heaviest weights.

Start with the seemingly unimportant choices – utilizing self-control to not take the last bite of the cake or forcing yourself to get out of bed and brush your teeth or making the decision to stop scrolling through social media before you really "feel" like you want to stop or making the small decision not to spit out a mean statement to someone when they provoke you. All of these things can occur in completely different areas of your life, but they all utilize the same self-control muscle. They all force you to take an action that goes against your emotions.

As you do these things on a regular basis, your self-control muscle will grow and having the strength and stamina to exercise that self-control in the larger decisions of your life will become possible.

THE SCIENCE OF SELF-CONTROL

In chapter 3, we referenced studies that revealed that "intense, prolonged, or repeated mental/neural activity – especially if it is conscious – will leave an enduring imprint in neural structure, like a surging current reshaping a riverbed....mental states become neural traits. Day after day, your mind is building your brain."[2] These neural channels create the path of where your thoughts naturally take you by default. These channels can be reshaped, but in order to do so it takes intentionality and - you guessed it, self-control.

Think of your brain as a snow sled on a snowy hill. When the snow on that hill is fresh and you put your sled at the top, you can direct your sled anywhere. You can shape your own path. But each time you sled down that hill utilizing that same snow path, the deeper and more set that path becomes. If it continues to snow and that fresh snow continues to build up the walls of that path while you continue sledding, that path becomes even more concrete.

If you decided that you wanted to use a less-used path or create a new path altogether, you could no longer just let the sled go where it wants to go by default. If the site of the new path was close in proximity to the established path, you may find yourself constantly defaulting to the more established path and have to stop your ride down the hill mid-slide and readjust. This entire process would take intentional effort and as we've said repeatedly, it's not the path of least resistance. But after the new path is established, that new path becomes the new default. That intentionally-built path becomes your new "natural."

This is the same way our brain works in regards to our thoughts, feelings and beliefs. The trait that keeps us from going down the default path and forge a new path is self-control. Self-control by definition is "restraint exercised over one's own impulses, emotions, or desires."[3] Without self-control, a new path cannot be forged.

SELF-CONTROL FOR SPIRITUAL GROWTH

Self-control isn't just a practical admonition. It's also the key component in carrying out the instructions in God's Word for how we gain victory in our lives over thoughts, emotions and temptations.

Going back to our dog metaphor in the last chapter, we understand that in order to have a stronger dogwalker (spirit) walking a small, manageable dog (soul), we need to feed our spirit and starve our flesh. Flesh in this context refers to our biological urges, mind, will and emotions apart from God's Will.

In order to carry this mandate out, there are practical decisions that we need to make in our daily lives that require more self-control.

STARVE YOUR FLESH

When we talk about "starving your flesh," we are discussing the daily practice of a life that is already surrendered to God and thus, needs to be exercised regularly.

Spend a few minutes taking an inventory of the things that feed your flesh, then begin the process of starving your flesh of those things. If something catches your attention, don't let your eyes linger. If a pastime always leads to being overpowered with temptation, drop the pastime. If a thought enters your head, don't dwell on it – shift what you are thinking about. Find some accountability with this to help with the journey.

It starts with small morsels of starvation – the little "wins." Even when you don't feel like a small decision matters, every opportunity that you have to deny your flesh of what you know is not in alignment with God's Word, you are slowly starving your flesh. This is one of the reasons that fasting is so incredibly powerful. It's an opportunity to go above and beyond our normal "right" decisions and completely deplete our flesh of its life source – food. If your flesh is already weak, then fasting is a way to make sure it's good and dead. If your flesh needs to be weakened, then fasting will give you a strong start on your journey. If fasting is a new concept for you, then we highly recommend the book "Fasting" by Jentezen Franklin.[4]

The more you starve your flesh the weaker it becomes until you achieve your victory. However, keep in mind, just like a dog that is being starved, your flesh might get weaker but at some point - just before it dies - it will have one fight left. It rallies for one major fight because it refuses to die. So don't become complacent. You must continue starving your flesh and give it no ground. When that last fight comes, and your spirit maintains the stance of strength, your flesh (in that particular area of your mind, will, and emotions) will finally die.

FEED YOUR SPIRIT

It doesn't do you much good to have a weak flesh and still have a weak spirit. You cannot find victory by only dying to yourself. Victory is found when you live in Christ.

Traditional spiritual disciplines are what strengthen your spirit. These things are often overlooked as religious or unnecessary but they are the only ways to strengthen your spirit. Prayer, reading your Bible, fasting and worship – these are things that draw you closer to your spirit's life source – God.

Another important but less popular discipline is obedience. Every opportunity for obedience to God and His Word is an invitation into intimacy. It's you making a choice to deny the flesh for the sake of Christ. Even the small acts of obedience are rewarded by the strengthening of your spirit.

It may be a struggle to engage in these spiritual disciplines at first (because remember, your mind, will and emotions are easily swayed to support whichever part of you is stronger) and it may seem like nothing comes out of it, but keep going and slowly your spirit will grow.

Several years ago, God showed me (Robert) a powerful illustration and it has helped me in discipling many younger believers. Imagine that the process to spiritual intimacy with God happens along a cycle. At the top of the circle is obedience, then intimacy, then sensitivity, then finally, clarity before it circles back around to intimacy.

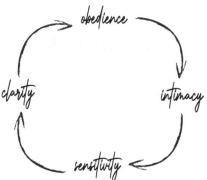

Obedience is always the priority. If you're going to live a victorious life, you're going to have to live a life of obedience. When we're obedient, we experience greater intimacy. When we have greater intimacy, we're going to be more sensitive to God and His Holy Spirit. When we're more sensitive, we're going to have greater clarity. When we have greater clarity, we'll know clearly what God is leading us to next and we'll have another opportunity for obedience.

Most Christians know they are "supposed" to pray, read the Bible and apply it in obedience and yet, they don't. This ends up being another example of a lack of knowledge. It's easy to dismiss the mandate to read the Word and pray when it's given as a religious instruction to be a "good Christian." But the truth is that reading the Bible and praying as a religious task to check off your to-do list will rarely get you the results you are looking for.

That's because those spiritual disciplines are not intended to be religious legalism but rather, tools to be used in building a personal relationship with God. It's difficult to build a relationship with someone that you never talk to or know anything about. Likewise, it's difficult to get the promises of victory that you hear about if you don't actually know what the Bible instructs in order to get those promises.

DOES IT REALLY MAKE A DIFFERENCE?

I (Gloria) equate this scenario to how I viewed my water intake for most of my life. Everyone knows the health benefits of drinking enough water. I research everything (learning is a passion), so I had all the knowledge of how much water can benefit you.

On top of that, for years I suffered from extreme fatigue, depression and mental cloudiness and no matter how much sleep I got, I'd last for a couple hours and then fall back into lethargy. I had been repeatedly told all my life after every medical test that I was severely dehydrated. And yet, I never made drinking enough water a priority. Many people would consider that stupidity. In hindsight, it was stupidity, but it was deeper than that - it was unbelief.

It's not like I didn't have water accessible to me. I certainly had the head knowledge of the benefits and as busy as I always say I am, I had time to drink water all day if I were intentional about it. The solution to my fatigue was readily available and I knew about it. But full transparency, I just didn't think it was really going to make that big of a difference. During that time, I was suffering from an autoimmune disease (which God healed me from but that's a story for another day) and I used that disease to explain all of my ailments and it became a crutch to excuse myself from doing what I was able to do in attempting to diminish some of the ailments.

But then God healed me of the disease from the inside out and although most of the symptoms ceased, I still found myself incredibly fatigued and weak most of the time. So then I chalked it up to simply being a mom of three small children, running a ministry, working on high-demand projects, managing the house and waking up at 5am every morning to get my Jesus time in – those things would wear any person out. And fatigue became a constant complaint in our house – I just really wanted to sleep all the time.

Finally, after Robert told me about how much energy he had after drinking copious amounts of water, I decided to give it a shot. And lo and behold! The next day I woke up at 5am without the help of snooze and had energy the entire day. I was still tired – the water didn't cancel out my need for sleep – but there is a difference between being tired and being fatigued and I wasn't fatigued.

I cried literal tears because of how much of a difference it made. I cried tears because of all the days that I missed out on that energy simply because I didn't drink what was already available to me.

I imagine that's how many Christians are. Just like I had the head knowledge of the benefits of water and I had the water, Christians have the knowledge of the many benefits of God's Word and they have God's Word and carry it around with them and might drink some of God's presence on Sunday morning – but then neglect it the rest of the week. And then they wonder why they aren't experiencing all this "joy," "peace," "victory" and "promises" that Christians are supposed to have. And it's usually because they aren't drinking the water of God's presence daily.

If you don't drink water every day, you won't get the benefits of water. It's really simple. And the reason I didn't drink the water is because I didn't believe it was going to make that big of a difference. The reason most Christians don't spend time with God every day is because they don't really, truly, genuinely believe it's going to make that big of a difference in their lives.

They are content to go to church on Sundays and get an encouraging word and then live the rest of the week making the best decisions they can based on their emotions and their own logic and then they need constant encouragement every Sunday with no real sign of victorious or abundant living beyond their circumstances.

But friend let me tell you, it's not just about being able to make decisions based on God's Word, it's about having a personal, intimate relationship with Him. We, as humans, can only go so far. Even with all the knowledge of the Bible, we are still lacking if we do not have His presence in our lives. A personal relationship with God, where you sit down and spend time with Him on a daily basis, is what gives you the right perspective and the strength to carry out what is necessary to get your victory. You can implement all the self-control you want, but without God's presence, you will only get so far.

God is the one who carries you that extra mile to victory when you've gone as far as you can go within your own efforts. The real question is, do you really believe that spending time with Him every day will make that big of a difference?

PITFALLS OF SELF-CONTROL

You cannot have victory without self-control but you cannot get victory with self-control alone. As we emphasize the value of self-control, we also want to explain the difference between suppressing your thoughts and emotions and releasing them. Suppressing your emotions without release can wreak havoc on your physical, mental and spiritual health.[5] It is not God's desire for us to suppress who we really are or how we really feel and simply "behave" correctly externally – that is called behavior modification.

For the most part, behavior modification and self-control are the same thing. Behavior modification is when we adjust our behavior but nothing more. Like self-control, it's what prevents us from acting out impulsively in the moment or for a short season as we process what needs to be adjusted internally. However, if we stay in a state of behavior modification and it never moves into heart modification, we'll become toxic to ourselves and others.

God calls us to adjust the attitude and perspective of our hearts to align with His Truth – this is heart modification. It's when we adjust the attitudes of our hearts that we no longer have to intentionally modify our behavior – but our behavior flows out of our repositioned hearts. Eventually, what is only heart modification becomes God forming Christ in us and we then have a heart transformation. This is when our spirit has gained complete control of our souls and our bodies in a specific area of our lives. True transformation can only come from God.

Self-control is a tool that we utilize while we trust that God's ways are higher than our own. Self-control is not something we force on ourselves in order to prove that we are good enough to be loved by God. The truth is that God already loves you and if you've given your life to Him, then He already sees you as approved and accepted.

Therefore, self-control is not just a religious act of suppressing who we are or how we feel. Rather, it's a pause button on our emotions in a moment that allows God the opportunity to work out the situation according to His will and protect us from suffering the consequences of acting out rashly based on our emotions.

In exercising Godly self-control - although we may modify our behavior in that moment - we also have to follow-up with releasing whatever we are feeling to God. 1 Peter 5:7 says to "cast all your anxiety on Him, because He cares about you" and in Philippians 4:6 it says "in everything by prayer and pleading with thanksgiving let your requests be made know to God." It is through prayer that we are able to ensure that we aren't just suppressing how we feel to our detriment but that we are releasing it to God for our healing.

Once we've released it to God, we then must allow Him to change our hearts, attitudes and perspectives on the situation. That adjustment may mean having more grace for other people because of how much grace God has given us. It may mean knowing that ultimately our lives are in God's hands and there is no human that can dislike us or wrong us enough that will cause God's plan for our lives to foil – and the only way out of His hands is in our own disobedience or to remain in unforgiveness and offense. The heart adjustment may be in truly believing the truth about who you are in Christ and finally being able to identify the lies. God is multi-faceted and personal – if you will take the time to listen, whatever He reveals to you will be just what you need to grow in that moment.

In discussing self-control we can fall into two extreme groups of people. Many Christians who desire to follow religious "rules" and depend exclusively on their ability to exercise self-control, end up suppressing their thoughts and emotions and become legalistic and judgmental. On the other end of the spectrum, the world teaches us to accept everything we feel and think without question and not to exercise self-control at all and end up living destructive lives as emotional tornadoes. But God calls us to release our thoughts and emotions to Him so He can heal them and transform us in the process.

This process is no different than the process of giving our lives over to God in salvation:

1. Hear and believe the gospel of Truth

2. Recognize and confess our sinful state and confess

3. Turn away from our old life (i.e. repent)

4. Surrender to God through Jesus as our Lord (the ultimate authority in our lives) and Savior (the one who rescues us)

5. Declare publicly that we are a new creation in Christ

6. Follow God in obedience as He directs us through our daily pursuit of Him

Likewise, releasing deceitful thoughts and emotions follow the same steps:

1. Hear and believe the scriptural Truth as it relates to that area of our thoughts and emotions

2. Recognize the lies and confess without restraint to God the thoughts and emotions we are struggling with (He knows everything anyway, so this step is to usher us into our healing process)

3. Anytime those negative thoughts or emotions make an appearance, don't dwell on them or accept them; but rather, resist the devil (i.e. turn away from them)

4. Determine in our minds and hearts that although we may feel or think differently, we will still choose to trust that God will realign our souls with His Spirit as we move forward in obedience to His Word

5. Speak the Truth into the situation rather than the opposing thoughts or feelings (i.e. instead of declaring "I'm worried about my kids", state "God loves my children more than I do and He will protect them"; instead of stating "I'm depressed", state "I'm thankful that God has provided for me everything I need"; instead of stating "I'm worthless", state "I am fearfully and wonderfully made", etc. This isn't about denying your current state of mind, it's about choosing to vocalize what God says about your situation rather than letting your thoughts and emotions stand-alone unchallenged).

6. Continue to spend time in God's presence daily and go wherever He directs.

A simple way of remembering this process is to "confess, repent and place faith." You are confessing what thoughts and emotions are lies, repenting or "turning away from" them and turning back to God by declaring the Truth. Then you are placing faith in God and His ability to forgive and heal that area of your life. Confess, repent and place faith. It's in following this process in every situation that occurs in your thoughts and emotions that you will receive your victory.

This doesn't work instantly or overnight, but it does work. As you continue to push through this process, your soul (what you think and feel) will eventually line up with your Spirit and you will feel a fuller and deeper sense of being exactly who God created you to be – not because you suppressed how you really feel, but because you released who you feel you are and allowed God to transform you into who He created you to be.

\\ **IF YOU WANT A VICTORIOUS LIFE, YOU HAVE TO LIVE AN OBEDIENT LIFE.**

\\ 5
POWER TO OVERCOME

"For our struggle is not against flesh and blood, but against the rulers, against the powers, against the world forces of this darkness, against the spiritual forces of wickedness in the heavenly places."

Ephesians 6:12

Jesus tells us in Matthew 26:41 to "keep watching and praying so that you do not come into temptation; the spirit is willing, but the flesh is weak." Essentially what Jesus is telling us is that our Spirit is always in agreement with the will of God and our flesh is always in opposition and the only way to bring them into alignment is through prayer which is drawing us into a deeper and more intimate relationship with God by strengthening our spirit, making it possible to bring our flesh into submission.

There are two parts to "bringing your flesh into submission": the bringing and the submitting. Just like "the body without the spirit is dead, so also faith without works is dead" (Jm. 2:26). Everything in our relationship with God requires us to both do what we can in our own strength and to trust in God for the things that are beyond our capabilities. The latter part is what happens in the supernatural realm that we cannot control. In order to fully bring your mind, will and emotions to God, there has to be a submission to God in all things first so that spiritually, your physical efforts can produce results. Without a heart that is fully surrendered to God, you will only "labor in vain" (Ps. 127:1).

COMPLETE SURRENDER

Ephesians 4:26-27 states "be angry, and yet do not sin; do not let the sun go down on your anger, and do not give the devil an opportunity." Before you can effectively resist the enemy, you have to make sure that you aren't the one actually inviting the enemy to wreak havoc in your soul.

Usually, this type of invitation occurs because there is an area of sin in your life. These sins go beyond the daily practice of starving your flesh because they are areas that you are unwilling to surrender to God.

We encourage you to take a moment to step back and ask God to reveal to you any areas of your life that you have refused to surrender to Him. Some examples may be refusing to forgive someone that hurt you deeply or holding offense against someone. It can be the practice of sexual activity outside of marriage, refusing to honor the authority in your life (whether that be family, spiritual, career or governmental authorities) or it can be a belief system that refuses to believe that opinions and emotions do not supersede God's Truth. It could also be something else entirely.

Knowing that God's promises and victories are always attached to an instruction of surrender, you'll need to take seriously the fact that disobedience could be allowing the enemy to steal the victory that God has already given you. Remember that the three parts of your being (spirit, soul, body) are all interconnected – but not necessarily in a way that makes sense to us. Disobedience in one area of your life can block your breakthrough in an entirely different area of your life. Disobedience in your finances can block a breakthrough in your relationships. Disobedience in honoring authority can block a breakthrough in your peace and so on.

This doesn't mean that you need to be perfect in every area of your life to receive the promise of victory, but it does mean that - even if you have to struggle through the process - you do need to have a heart that is willing to allow God to take you through that process. God's not looking for perfection here, He's looking for a willingness to surrender. It's the difference between someone stating, "I will never forgive that person" and instead saying "I am trying to forgive that person, but it's a struggle."

RESISTING THE ENEMY

As we've already discussed, the part that requires our effort is dependent heavily on our ability to exercise self-control. It's not about utilizing self-control to make yourself feel or think a certain way – the actual onset of permanently thinking and feeling differently is the portion of the process that God handles through your obedience and prayer.

If you have enough self-control, you can "fake it 'till you make it" and sometimes that is a necessary part of the process, but it is also a temporary part of the process. Real victory comes when your emotions and your thoughts are in line with God's Word without a daily effort. What you do need self-control for is preparing the way for God to change how we feel and think. James 4:7 says "resist the devil, and he will flee from you."

You can't "resist the enemy" if you don't know when it's the enemy. If you aren't spending time in God's Word, you won't know what the truth is and be able to determine what the lies are. Once you know the truth, you then have to actually believe the truth. Knowing is one thing, believing is another.

Once you believe the truth and understand the lie, you have to stop allowing the lie to sit in your mind. It's not enough to ignore the lie or attempt to stop thinking about the lie. You have to actively resist the lie. That is not a passive action. You cannot spend all your time complaining to God that you don't want to think or feel a certain way anymore while yet refusing to put in the mental effort that you have available (no matter how small that amount may be) to resist those same negative thoughts and emotions and replace them with truth.

ARE YOU REALLY RESISTING?

The word "resist" reminds me (Gloria) of an incident that happened on my 17th birthday. A couple of my best friends got dressed up and took me out for dinner at a local Italian restaurant. We had parked in the back of the parking lot behind a dumpster because that's where one of my best friends and her boyfriend had their first kiss – so now it was tradition to park in that spot every time they went out to eat there.

The dinner went well and we were all having a great time - until we were walking back to our car late that night. In the parking lot, illuminated only by a few remaining parking lot lights, I thought I saw something moving behind the dumpster. I stopped in my tracks and didn't want to keep walking but my friends convinced me it was probably just an animal or something, so we continued walking towards the car.

But as we passed the dumpster, several men dressed in all black and with black ski masks on came out from behind the dumpster and covered our mouths with cloths that had a distinct scent to it. It was disorienting and I couldn't process what was happening until I heard one of the men exclaim, "why isn't it working on her?" As I struggled to get free, I was able to catch glimpses of my other two friends passed out on the ground and being carried away.

Even as I write this more than two decades later, my heart still races as I detail those moments. Eventually (and by eventually, I mean probably seconds later), the men abandoned the idea of trying to make me pass out and gathered around to pick me up and try to get me in a car kicking and screaming. And kicking and screaming I did.

I literally fought for my life. They say your life flashes before your eyes when you are about to die and I can attest to that. I truly believed I was about to die (or worse) and while I was fighting, dozens of moving images flashed across my mind seemingly at the same time. I thought of all my most cherished memories from my childhood. I thought of my parents and my siblings. I thought of my friends. Then I thought about the different scenarios of what would happen to me next if I didn't win this fight. I thought of all the things that I wouldn't get to experience – getting married, having a family, seeing my dreams come true. I thought of what could be going on in the kitchen of the restaurant that I could be screaming so loudly and no one was coming out to rescue me. I wondered why I didn't have enough faith to scream the name of Jesus and if in this moment I was really that concerned about embarrassing myself. And as I grew tired of fighting, biting, kicking and screaming, I slowed down for a split second. Then I saw my funeral and my parents mourning and I saw from my coffin looking up, my sister crying over my death and leaving her behind. And that image gave me the strength to keep fighting.

By this time, I was laid across the back seat with someone fighting to push my feet inside the driver's side door and a couple others fighting to get my head inside the passenger side door. I fought for what seemed like an eternity. Everything in slow motion.

As it seemed like the fight was coming to an end, I reared my head backwards and I saw a person with a video camera recording the entire incident. Then my mind was flooded with fear of what kind of people these were and their evil intentions and if the torture that awaited me was worse than death itself. And then the camera person yelled "Stop! That's enough." And everything stopped.

Absolutely frantic, I scrambled out of the car as my friends appeared - fully conscious - and my masked captors revealed that they were some of my closest friends – and this was all an attempt to take me to my surprise birthday party. As my mind started to process what had just happened, I think every emotion known to man flooded through my body and exploded in anger through many choice words that I won't repeat here.

After I had calmed down, relief and gratitude that it was "just a joke" flooded my being and I cried for hours into the night before I finally fell asleep. It may have been a joke to everyone else, but to me, it was all very real.

My friends gave me the VHS of the incident and after several weeks I gathered up the courage to watch it. In the beginning of the recording they "rehearsed" the kidnapping. They jumped out from behind the dumpster, grabbed my stand-in on both sides and casually walked me into the car. Smooth as butter.

I was bewildered at the thought that these people would assume that I would believe I was being kidnapped and think that I would just cooperate without any sign of resistance. Who would do that? Who would know that someone was trying to destroy their life and yet walk alongside them, hands bound, to their death without so much as an attempt for freedom?

And yet, that's exactly where many of us find ourselves in our thoughts and our emotions. We see the enemy come in with these lies, these worries, these feelings that don't line up with God's Word, these elements that we know will ultimately lead us to destruction and yet we follow alongside them wherever they want to take us without a peep.

That's not resistance. If you believed that every lie, every wrong thought and every destructive emotion was an attempt on your life, I'd think that those things are worth a fight. Those things are worth the effort of resistance. That's what scripture is calling us to do. He's not calling us to casually proclaim to our captor unenthusiastically, "Oh no! Don't take me. I don't want to go." While we walk with them step-by-step away from the promises God has given us. No! God is telling us to resist the enemy! Resist – fight for what's yours – and what is yours is your right to choose what you think and what you feel.

The devil doesn't get to tell you how to feel and your flesh doesn't get to tell you what to think about. You are in charge of you and the only one that you should be relinquishing that control to is God Almighty, your Loving Creator.

SAY IT OUT LOUD

Once you understand that you are not fighting against yourself but against an enemy that has convinced you that you don't have any control of your thoughts and emotions, then it's time to start utilizing the weapons at your disposal.

Hebrews 4:12 says "the word of God is living and active, and sharper than any two-edged sword" and Proverbs 12:18 states that "the words of the reckless pierce like swords, but the tongue of the wise brings healing." Anything in reference to the tongue represents the audible vocalization of your words. Proverbs doesn't say that the thoughts of the wise bring healing – it says that "the tongue of the wise brings healing." The words that you choose to vocalize can either bring death to yourself and to others or by speaking the Word of God you can bring death to the lies of the enemy and life to the truth of God.

It is what actually, audibly comes out of your mouth that brings life or death. I used to think that Christians who walked around audibly renouncing things and claiming things were super-spiritual and it was just a cheesy religious show – and so I never really implemented that practice. But the older I got the more I realized that there is great effectiveness to this practice.

For one, God alone knows every human heart (1 Kgs. 8:39). So "resisting the devil" in your mind might help you, but you double the effectiveness when you let the devil hear you resist him. Much like a captor taking a captive who resists physically, but also resists audibly – it reinforces the level of resistance.

When I (Gloria) was dealing with my depression, the deliverance happened within a matter of a couple weeks and it was because I implemented two things with consistent force: I fought and I fought audibly. Nothing changed until I finally got a fight in me. I decided that I didn't want to spend my days neglecting life and thinking of ways to kill myself – God promised me an abundant life and I got angry that there was an enemy out there trying to steal if from me and steal me from my family. I got angry at the depression. I stopped believing that the depression was who I was and I separated myself into a different entity and I started getting mad at the enemy and the enemy's depression that he was trying to put on me. I got a fight in my spirit.

Once I got the fight, I told God, "God, I'm going to fight this, but you have to help me. If you are real, help me." It's important to remember that we aren't able to do it all in our own strength, but it's God's grace that bridges the gap from where our strength ends to where the promises begin. It's our job to take the steps that we can take in obedience and it's God who carries us the rest of the way – it takes both our self-control and our prayers to activate results.

The day I was delivered, I sat up in my bed, I said my prayer declaring war on my depression and I went straight to the kitchen to do the dishes. I don't know why I went to the kitchen except perhaps it was the first productive thing I could think of. From there, every time a negative thought or a negative emotion started to overwhelm me I would audibly declare, "Stop!! I will not even finish that thought!" I did this continually for a couple days and slowly over the next couple weeks the depression broke completely off of me. Although I've still had sad days and difficult seasons, I haven't dealt with suicidal thoughts or depression since.

It wasn't until I read Neil T. Anderson's book, "The Bondage Breaker" that I had a fuller grasp of what occurred during my breakthrough several years earlier. Now being able to put the power of renouncing the lie and declaring the truth into context, it has become a staple process in my house with my three children. Every time they declare a lie or anything negative, they immediately know that I will make them audibly renounce it and then declare the scripture that combats whatever lie they just said. For instance, if they say "this is a horrible day", they renounce it and then they follow it up with "because 'this is the day which the Lord has made; let's rejoice and be glad in it." (Ps. 118:24)

I have to laugh at myself every time it happens because I can just imagine my 20-something year old self burying her face in her hands embarrassed at the weird cheesy Christian scene playing out in my house these days. But I guess at some point in your life you have to ask yourself if you really believe the Word of God and if so, are you going to let discomfort or inconvenience in doing something keep you from experiencing all the promises of God? If you want the promises, you actually have to actively do what God tells you to do.

ROBERT'S STORY

I (Robert) experienced my own battle with anxiety and depression through hypochondria. This was extremely out of character for me. Most of my life, up until that point, I had been a strong-willed, strong-minded person. I was usually very much in control - to a fault - of my thoughts and emotions. Even to the point that I felt like people who struggled with depression and anxiety were simply not very strong or mature. I clearly had a lot of growing to do.

One typical morning I woke up and went to the restroom to blow my nose and noticed some blood on the tissue. Any other day, this would have been no big deal. I would have brushed it off and moved on about my day. But for some reason, the enemy knew there was something different about that day. Maybe I was in a weakened state spiritually - who knows, but the enemy got my number. So, like any sane person would do, I took to google to figure out what my symptoms meant (don't do that) and after 10-minutes I went from simply having dry skin to dying of some disease.

The enemy had convinced me that I was sick and that's all it took. I was like a snowball going downhill at 100mph. After a few days, I started having night sweats, after a month I had lost 10lbs and after 3 months I had lost 30lbs. I was experiencing spasms and twitches in my muscles due to the stress I was experiencing regarding my "impending death." It got so bad that I couldn't even play with my kids because I was so paralyzed with the thoughts of how they would move on without me or who would play with them when I was gone. I would wake up in the middle of the night drenched and my bed soaked from panicking in my sleep. The enemy was winning this battle in my mental health.

After about 10-months of this, I could no longer take it. I verbally got angry. I began to yell back at the enemy "look, I'm still here." I began to literally shout scripture at myself and the enemy. I might have looked or sounded crazy to anyone walking by my home, but I got to the point of such desperation that I was no longer going to live in this paralyzed state. I verbally, mentally and spiritually resisted the devil. After that, things began to improve.

I wish I could say it was instantaneous and complete healing - but it wasn't. Unlike Gloria's fairly immediate deliverance, my victory came more gradually. It took about 2-months of this battle. Yet with each victory, I celebrated. I celebrated another day, I celebrated my response of scripture instead of fear. I celebrated simply being alive and being strengthened by God. I celebrated God's promises over my life. All audibly. Remember, the enemy needs to HEAR your resistance.

After a year of mental hell, the loss of 30lbs, countless sleepless nights, crippling fear and torment, I finally broke free. By the power of God, and the evidence of His faithfulness and fulfilled biblical promises, I was set free. I have now been over six years without a single sleepless night or real battle with anxiety. I do believe a couple times - maybe two or three - the enemy has shown up and tried to "test the waters" and a weight or anxious feeling would hit. But now my faith has been so built up that I've been able to quickly reject those feelings, replace them with God's promises and truth and the attack subsides almost immediately. Those are moments of temptation. No, not the temptation for a sin I might enjoy but instead it's a temptation to shift my focus from God and His faithfulness to fear, doubt and worry. It's a temptation to trust in something - or anything - greater than I trust in God.

OVERCOMING TEMPTATION

Often times we think of temptations as the seductress drawing us into the bed with her or the fresh donut on the table calling our name. But let's go a little deeper with this and consider that every wayward thought or negative mood is also a temptation to take us down a road we don't really want to go down.

In studying the temptations that Christ endured during His time in the wilderness, we have found striking similarities to what Jesus was being tempted with at the core and what we are tempted with on a daily basis. It's not just an outdated story of an encounter with the Devil. It's a modern-day playbook of how to live a life of victory in a world of temptations.

Lust of the Flesh

"Then Jesus was led up by the Spirit into the wilderness to be tempted by the devil. And after He had fasted for forty days and forty nights, He then became hungry. And the tempter came and said to Him, "If You are the Son of God, command that these stones become bread." But He answered and said, "It is written: 'Man shall not live on bread alone, but on every word that comes out of the mouth of God.'"
Matthew 4:1-4

When Jesus was led into the wilderness to be tempted, the first temptation He encountered was in relation to the desires of His flesh – food and water.

This represents all the things in life that we need to survive. It would include things we need to survive physically like food and water. It includes things we need for our human race to survive and for connection, like sex. And it includes things that we need emotionally to live an abundant life, like passion.

These basic needs are not inherently evil when they are used as tools to assist us in furthering our obedience to Christ. In fact, these things are blessings from God for us to enjoy and be able to experience fullness of life – within the boundaries He has established in His Word.

If food becomes an obsession, it can derail your physical health. If sex happens outside of marriage, it can derail the health of your worth and relationships. If your desire to "feel alive" becomes your solitary pursuit, it can become an emotional addiction as detrimental to your emotional health as substance abuse is to your physical health. That's when these things - that God intended to add value to our lives - move to being objects that overtake our lives instead and they become temptations we have to resist.

Matthew 4:4 says that when presented with temptations of the flesh, Jesus replied "Man shall not live on bread alone, but on every Word that comes from the mouth of God." He wasn't saying that we should never eat bread or that bread was somehow wrong. He's saying that bread is not our God. It is not the thing that we live for or that we can allow to control our decisions. Bread is not what gives us everlasting life, it is a tool to sustain us in our earthly life and it needs to be put under subjection to God's Word.

When Jesus was called to fast, He was called to abstain from food or water during that time. That didn't mean that He was never to eat or drink again, it meant that He was more obedient to God than He was to his body's desires and needs.

In the same way, you cannot allow your sexual urges to lead you into decisions outside of God's Word. You cannot allow your emotional desires – whether they be positive emotional "highs" or negative emotional "lows" to dictate how you proceed throughout the day.

Just like an individual who is controlled by their desire for food will become morbidly obese suffering a wide array of health problems that prohibit them from truly enjoying their life, so will an individual controlled by their emotions or desire for sex also suffer a wide array of dysfunctions that will prohibit them from having life more abundantly.

Sex was given as a gift for a husband and his wife to celebrate their union and to procreate. Emotions were given as a gift to allow us to experience life's events more fully. But they both have to be submitted to God's Word because our needs are not only met by the products of this earth but more-so by the understanding and obedience of scripture.

Lust of the Eyes

"Again, the devil took Him along to a very high mountain and showed Him all the kingdoms of the world and their glory; and he said to Him, "All these things I will give You, if You fall down and worship me." Then Jesus said to him, "Go away, Satan! For it is written: 'You shall worship the Lord your God, and serve Him only." Then the devil left Him; and behold, angels came and began to serve Him."
Matthew 4:8-11

When Jesus was placed on the mountain and shown all that He could have, His experience directly corresponds with everything that we see and would like to have. From cars to houses to jobs and people – it's everything that embodies a materialistic world of being able to have whatever you want.

Matthew 13:22 talks of seed that falls "among the thorns, this is the one who hears the word, and the anxiety of the world and the deceitfulness of wealth choke the word, and it becomes unfruitful." In other words, there are well-meaning Christians that start off right but their ambitions to have things (accolades and applause) become their idol. Instead of worshipping God, they worship their possessions.

This idolization can also extend to our pursuit of happiness. We can desire to feel happy so much that we do whatever we feel is necessary to give us moments of temporary happiness. But Jesus reminds us that we should "worship the Lord your God, and serve Him only" (Mt. 4:10).

Especially in our current culture of mental health awareness and self-care, we can get distracted from worshipping God by focusing all our energy on protecting our happiness and our peace. We set up more boundaries, take more time to care for ourselves and work our way down a checklist of things professionals tell us will make us happy – get more sun, eat healthy, get better sleep, take time for yourself, do something you enjoy, etc.

There's nothing wrong with any of these things. In fact, Genesis 2:3 tells us that "God blessed the seventh day and sanctified it, because on it He rested from all His work." But when Jesus tells us that loving God and loving others are the two greatest commandments (Mt. 22:36-40) and we insert "love yourself" in between those two – we've determined that our pursuit of our own happiness is more important than our pursuit of God and His will. And His will says to put others above ourselves.

We understand the argument that in order to love others, you must love yourself because you cannot give what you do not have. There is truth to this – if you are in despair you certainly cannot help someone else out of their despair. We are not saying that having stability in your value in Christ is not imperative to being able to "love your neighbor as yourself." However - as with most cultural beliefs - what started as a positive movement to help people realize their value has turned into a negative culture of people selfishly placing their wants and needs above other people. "Loving yourself" in the context of Godly value is important, but the method and motivation in how we come to love ourselves needs to be clarified.

The Kingdom of God is a world of paradoxes. We give and therefore we receive (Pr. 3:9-10). We place ourselves last to become first (Mk. 10:44). In our humility we are exalted (1 Pt. 5:6). We lose our life in order to gain it (Mk. 8:35).

We cannot learn to love ourselves by focusing more on ourselves. God is love (1 Jn. 4:8) and it's only by focusing more on God that we can love ourselves and love others. We're not teaching that self-care is bad - we're teaching that any and all strength, peace, rest and happiness are fruits of serving God, not ourselves. The focus has to shift from us to God and others.

Sadly, culturally, we've decided in our own human understanding that the way to a peaceful and happy life is to take care of ourselves first. By placing our own pursuit of happiness above our obedience to God, we are in fact, falling into the lust of the eyes. We see happiness, we want it, we decide to get it by adjusting our priorities in opposition from what God has directed.

But "you shall worship the Lord your God, and serve Him only" (Mt. 4:10). We don't worship things or accolades. And we don't worship happiness. And we certainly don't worship ourselves. We worship God and in doing so, God will give us peace, "which surpasses all comprehension" (Pp. 4:7).

Pride of Life

"Then the devil took Him along into the holy city and had Him stand on the pinnacle of the temple, and he said to Him, "If You are the Son of God, throw Yourself down; for it is written: 'He will give His angels orders concerning You'; and 'On their hands they will lift You up, so that You do not strike Your foot against a stone.'"
Jesus said to him, "On the other hand, it is written: 'You shall not put the Lord your God to the test."
Matthew 4:5-7

In Jesus' case, He was taken to a cliff and tempted to throw Himself down and test God's protection. It is true that God promised His protection, but if Jesus could do as He wished and take advantage of God's promises, then He would be placing Himself above God – pride.

We do the same thing when we "test" God. It's when we feel that we have come to a point in our life physically, financially, spiritually, etc., that we are untouchable or we cannot fail. We begin to play with fire and see how close we can get to sin without actually touching it. We tempt God.

This is the person who thinks they are so spiritually mature that they can flirt a little with someone else and aren't in danger of being unfaithful to their spouse. This is the person who thinks that they've "made it" financially and so they deserve to splurge on extravagant and risky purchases. It's the person who understands and believes that God will forgive them so they can entertain a little sin and ask for forgiveness later and still be OK with God. It's the person who thinks they are doing something so great that they can take advantage of people and treat them unkindly. It's the couple who are saving themselves for marriage and have been "doing good" and decide they can handle a short make-out session just this once.

There are an unlimited number of scenarios that exist. And we're sure that all of us can see glimpses of ourselves in even the few scenarios listed above. This is a life that's lived with pride – that's lived as though we are not capable of falling or are untouchable.

But the Christian life is not about seeing how close we can get to the line, it's about seeing how close we can get to God. When we start flirting with sin, we put ourselves in a situation where we can fall into sin purely by accident.

When our son, Urijah, was about 8-years-old, he had gotten some candy from school. We made it clear that he was not allowed to open the candy until he got home. But as we continued our drive, we could hear him twisting the ends of the clear wrapping around a Smarties candy open and then twisting them back closed. We reminded him that he would lose the candy entirely if he opened it in the car. He replied by exclaiming, "I'm not opening it, I just want to play with it."

Isn't that what so many of us do? We're not supposed to do something, but we get dangerously close. Instead of putting the candy away where it was guaranteed not to tempt him, Urijah chose to "flirt" with opening the candy. And in doing so, risked "accidentally" opening the package entirely and thereby losing the candy altogether.

But it's not really an accident is it? It feels like an accident because we don't intend to actually cross any lines, but we get so close that the line becomes blurred and then we really can't tell where we are in the process. We can tell you that even if you don't technically fall into sin, you certainly don't draw closer to God when you are inching towards the line.

The age-old debate regarding drinking alcohol as a sin is a perfect example of this. The Bible clearly states that getting drunk is a sin (Ga. 5:21). However, scripture does not explicitly state that drinking alcohol itself is a sin. This leads many in the Christian community to debate the sinfulness of moderate and social drinking. How does someone who chooses to drink alcohol know where the line is between having no impairment, being "buzzed" and being drunk? How do they know when they've crossed the line? And for what value? What value does drinking alcohol add to their life that they are willing to take such a risk to fall into disobedience and sin?

The greater question here may be why drinking alcohol is so important to a person that they are unwilling to lay it down to more fully pursue God – whether or not they "technically" are allowed to do something. 1 Corinthians 10:23 states that "all things are permitted, but not all things are of benefit." Wouldn't it be more beneficial for their walk with God, fulfilling their calling and positioning themselves to receive God's promises to walk as close to God as possible rather than walk as close to that blurred line of drunkenness as possible?

That's the thing about lines. Once you cross them, you've crossed it. You may not know when you crossed it. It can happen unintentionally almost as easily as it can happen intentionally. It's the pride of life that deceives us into believing that "it'll be ok."

But humility tells us that no matter how good our intentions are, we are all capable of falling given the right mix of circumstances. And knowing that, isn't it much wiser to set your personal boundaries significantly farther away from the actual line so that if you do accidentally trip over your own boundary, you are still safely contained on the right-side of the line?

This is what Jesus speaks of when He declares that "you shall not put the Lord your God to the test." God is not there at our beck and call. He is not obligated to forgive us, bless us and protect us every time we decide to make foolish decisions or tiptoe along the edge. God is a loving father. He forgives and redeems us when we turn away from our sins and surrender to Him. But it's never ok to take advantage of God's goodness.

Let's say you aren't concerned about needing God's forgiveness because you believe you are in total control of everything you do. That's another symptom of pride of life. Those who say they know how much they can handle or they know how close they can get are disillusioned in thinking that they control the fire.

You are in control of whether or not you play with the fire. That's it. You are not in control of whether or not someone decides to throw gas on the fire unexpectedly. You are not in control of the winds blowing the fire in a different direction. You are not in control of someone pushing you into the fire. To have so much pride as to think that you control all the circumstances of every situation you choose to test God in is exactly the temptation that this verse refers to. We combat that temptation by reminding ourselves that we are not in any kind of position to be testing God in any capacity.

VICTORY

These statements of truth from Matthew 4 – that we don't live for bread alone but on every Word that comes from God, that we worship God alone and we should never test God - these truths are what give us victory over every temptation in life.

"Man shall not live on bread alone, but on every Word that comes out of the mouth of God" (Mt. 4:4): Knowing and understanding the truth that our emotional impulses or moods and our negative thoughts are not our source of existence. But we live by the Word of God and He is our source in all things and our identity is established in Him. He gives us what we truly desire and He also gives us the tools, strategies and strength to exercise our authority over our thoughts and emotions.

"You shall worship the Lord your God, and serve Him only" (Mt. 4:10): As much as we may desire to be happy or fulfilled by whatever it is our thoughts and emotions lead us to, it is God who we worship and to Him alone our thoughts and emotions must come under subjection. He is faithful to bring our emotions and thoughts into alignment. When the temptation arrives to worship the negative moods that seem to overtake us, we worship God - not our depression or anxiety. When we are tempted to be anxious, we remind ourselves that we do not allow our anxieties to paralyze us but it is God who we worship and God who we serve and "a man's steps are ordained by the Lord" (Pr. 20:24). When we are tempted to stay in our depression, we remember that we do not dwell in those things that bring us down but rather on "whatever is pure, whatever is lovely, whatever is commendable, if there is any excellence and if anything worthy of praise, think about these things" (Pp. 4:8).

"You shall not put the Lord your God to the test" (Mt. 4:7): Ultimately, it's our humility before God that gives us the revelations we need to have victory in our lives. Understanding that we cannot control everything. In fact, we cannot control most things, but we are given the ability to control our own choices and we are given the ability to direct our minds and our hearts towards God.

SOUND MIND, SELF-CONTROLLED & SOBER IN PRAYER

> *"But the end of all things is near. Therefore be of sound mind, self-controlled, and sober in prayer."*
> *-1 Peter 4:7 (WEB)*

It's in 1 Peter 4:7 that we can clearly see the enemy's tactics in destroying God's children and their ability to have an abundant life.

Our time on this Earth is short. We, as Christians, have all of eternity to experience the blessings of God. But we only have a hundred years, at most, to make an impact on this Earth. We do not have time to waste it circling around the same mountain of our fleeting emotions and deceptive thoughts.

The urgency of our limited years is why we have to be even more diligent in making sure we have a sound mind, self-control and are sober in prayer. It's enlightening to us that it's in these three things that the enemy has deceived the church today in explosive numbers: mental stability (sound mind), self-denial (self-control) and intentional relationship (sober in prayer).

Having a sound mind means that we are not swayed by our own emotions or passions but that our perspective on things are through the lens of Truth and wisdom. Having self-control means that we are not consumed by this culture of focusing on ourselves first and doing whatever we want without restraint, but that we establish our Spirit's control over our soul so that our lives may be productive and bear fruit.

And most importantly, being sober in prayer means that we aren't reading our Bible and engaging in prayer as a means of religious rule-following but that we are being clear-minded and pure-hearted in our pursuit of God and what God desires for us.

It's in these three things: believing truth, exercising restraint and relationship with God that we realize that we actually can control the way we feel.

\\ **THE WORLD IS DESPERATE FOR HOPE AND WE HAVE IT. WE DO NOT HAVE TIME TO WASTE OUR LIVES CIRCLING THE SAME MOUNTAINS.**

OUR DEEPEST
APPRECIATION TO

*"Two are better than one because they
have a good return for their labor."*

Ecclesiastes 4:9

Our children, Urijah, Samuel and Liayah who have helped us practice verbalizing these revelations and have taught us many of these lessons in ways that you'll only know when you have grown into adults. Each of you forever represents God's Love towards us and we love you each dearly.

Our parents, John & Sarah Meyer and Merrie Brundage who have put up with us through decades of not understanding the revelations in this book and suffered many difficult seasons in our childhood as we grew (and continue to grow) in maturity.

Our pastors, Pastor Jentezen and Cherise Franklin, for the inspiration of witnessing first-hand your hearts for God, for the grace that you've extended to us through difficult seasons in learning these lessons and for your support in empowering us to fulfill God's call in our lives.

Our editor, Hannah Price, for working with us in communicating things more concisely and relevantly with laugh-out-loud notes and the numerous references to our "grandma" lingo. You make implementing your edits enjoyable and we appreciate how much better you make the book.

Our friend and "resident expert," Licensed Professional Counselor Amanda Walden, who took the time to review the content of this book from her professional perspective and experience and gave us much needed directon and encouragement! We appreciate you so much!

Most importantly, God our Father who quite literally changed our course with this book overnight and in doing so, flooded our minds and hearts with revelations and strategies that we only realized in hindsight after the book was finished. Although the delivery may be imperfect, the message is God's Word revealed throughout these pages. He truly is the one who deserves all the glory.

NOTES

Chapter 1: In the World

1. Encyclopedia.com. (n.d.). Art, Entertainment, And Propaganda. Retrieved 2021, July 30, from https://www.encyclopedia.com/history/educational-magazines/art-entertainment-and-propaganda.

2. Salt Lake Tribune. (2014, February 14). Love and Marriage: A History That Challenges The Notion of 'Traditional Marriage'. Huffpost. https://www.huffpost.com/entry/love-marriage-history_n_4774740#:~:text=The%20ideal%20of%20love%20as,personal%20happiness%2C%E2%80%9D%20Coontz%20said.

3. Spanglish. Directed by James L. Brooks. Los Angeles, CA: Sony Pictures, 2004. DVD.

Chapter 2: The Truth

1. Wikipedia. (n.d.). List of pedophile advocacy organizations. Retrieved 2021, July 30, from https://en.m.wikipedia. org/wiki/List_of_pedophile_advocacy_organizations.

2. Binazir, A. (2011, November 17). Addiction Recovery: Why We're Addicted to Negative Behaviors. Huffpost. https://www. huffpost.com/entry/addiction-recovery-why-we_b_603566.

Wood, P.B. (2008, May 8). Role of central dopamine in pain and analgesia. PubMed.gov. https:// pubmed.ncbi.nlm.nih.gov/18457535/.

3. NIDA. (2017, January 12). Tolerance, Dependence, Addiction: What's the Difference?. Retrieved from https://archives.drugabuse. gov/blog/post/tolerance-dependence-addiction-whats-difference.

4. Marks, J.W. (2021, June 3). Medical Definition of Neuroplasticity. MedicineNet. Retrieved from https:// www.medicinenet.com/neuroplasticity/definition. htm#:~:text=Neuroplasticity%3A%20The%20brain's%20 ability%20to,to%20changes%20in%20their%20environment.

5. Infidelity Recovery Institute. (n.d.). Affair Recovery Timeline. Retrieved 2021, July 30, from https://infidelityrecoveryinstitute. com/infidelity-101/affair-recovery-timeline/.

Chapter 3: Who You Are

1. Garća-Segura, L.M. (2009). Hormones and Brain Plasticity. Hormones and Brain Plasticity. 1-496. 10.1093/acprof:oso/9780195326611.001.0001.

2. Rossouw, J. (2017, March 8). How Neuroplasticity Changes the Brain. Linkedin. https://www.linkedin.com/pulse/how-neuroplasticity-changes-brain-jurie-rossouw

3. Newberg, A. and Waldman, M. (2012, August 1). Why This Word Is So Dangerous to Say or Hear. Psychology Today. https://www.psychologytoday.com/us/blog/words-can-change-your-brain/201208/why-word-is-so-dangerous-say-or-hear

4. MentalHealth360. (n.d.). Negative thoughts and beliefs. Retrieved 2021, July 30, from https://www.mindhealth360.com/contributor/negative-thought-patterns-and-beliefs/

Chapter 4: Self-Control Freak

1. Anderson, N. T. (2019). The Bondage Breaker. Harvest House Publishers.

2. Hanson, Rick. (2013, September 24). How to Grow the Good in your Brain. Greater Good Magazine. https://greatergood.berkeley.edu/article/item/how_to_grow_the_good_in_your_brain.

3. Merriam-Webster. (n.d.). self-control. Retrieved 2021, July 30, from https://www.merriam-webster.com/dictionary/self-control.

4. Franklin, J. (2007) Fasting. Charisma House.

5. Cousins, L.E. (2018, February). Are There Downsides to Always Trying to be Positive?. Health Agenda. https://www.hcf.com.au/health-agenda/body-mind/mental-health/downsides-to-always-being-positive.

COUNTERCULTURE MARRIAGE

Finding #happilyeverafter in a #marriagesucks world

Robert & Gloria Stella

#friendship #sex #romance #love #lust #honesty #priorities #communication #appreciation #expectations #money #arguing #respect #security #leadership #submission #commitment

We see relationship clichés unfold on the big screen, binge-watch dramas of failing marriages on TV, read about all the latest hook-ups and break-ups in the tabloids, indulge in fantasy romances in best-selling novels, nod our heads in agreement as we scroll through all the insulting memes about husbands, wives and marriage on our social media feed and stand around the watercooler cracking jokes about how much marriage sucks - and then we go home and wonder what happened to our happily ever after. If what we're doing isn't working, then it's time to do things differently.

With transparency and a real-life approach, Robert and Gloria take the truths in God's Word and deliver them with a fresh perspective for couples living in today's culture. Whether you're engaged or have decades of marriage under your belt, these timeless principles will lead you to a marriage the way God designed it to be - a good thing - filled with love, joy, peace, unity and purpose.

COUNTERCULTURE MARRIAGE WORKBOOK 2.0

Finding #happilyeverafter
in a #marriagesucks world

Robert & Gloria Stella

Topics include: #friendship #respect
#security #leadership #submission
#honesty #communication #money
#priorities #expectations #appreciation
#sex #romance #lust #love #commitment

The CounterCulture Marriage Workbook is a study guide that accompanies the book, CounterCulture Marriage. The workbook covers twelve culturally-relevant topics through short stories, fill-in-the-blank outlines, group discussion questions and self-evaluations.

THE LORD'S PRAYER FOR KIDS

Hannah Price & Gloria Stella
Illustrated by Eva Shoaf

A children's board book that translates the Lord's Prayer from Matthew 6 using child-friendly words and concepts - so children can not only memorize scripture, but truly understand it!